Town of Hadley

350TH ANNIVERSARY COMMEMORATIVE BOOK

A Publication of Hadley's 350th Celebration

MARY THAYER AND MARLA MILLER, EDITORS

WHITE RIVER PRESS
Amherst, Massachusetts

Town of Hadley 350th Commemorative Book

Copyright 2009 by Town of Hadley's 350th Committee,
Mary Thayer and Marla Miller, editors

No portion of this book may be reproduced or used in any form, or by any means, without prior written permission of the publisher

A publication of Hadley's 350th Celebration

White River Press
P.O. Box 3561
Amherst, MA 01004
www.whiteriverpress.com

Printed in the United States of America

ISBN: 978-1-935052-28-9 (hardcover)
ISBN: 978-1-935052-29-6 (softcover)

Book and cover design by Rebecca S. Neimark, Twenty-Six Letters

Library of Congress Cataloging-in-Publication Data

Town of Hadley 350th commemorative book : a publication of Hadley's 350th celebration / Mary Thayer and
   Marla Miller, editors.
      p. cm.
ISBN 978-1-935052-28-9 (hardcover : alk. paper) — ISBN 978-1-935052-29-6 (pbk. : alk. paper)
 1. Hadley (Mass. : Town)—Centennial celebrations, etc.—Pictorial works. I. Thayer, Mary, 1959–
   II. Miller, Marla R.
F74.H14T69 2009
974.4'23—dc22

2010012132

CONTENTS

History of Hadley	xvi
Introduction	xxi
350th Anniversary Events	xxiii

Winter

Snow and Ice Dinner Dance	2
Hadley Village Music Concert Series	4
The Souvenir Shoppe	6
Publications	10
Hadley Historical Commission Activities	12
Hopkins Academy	15

Spring

Girl Scout History Fair	18
Farm Tours: Montgomery Rose and North Hadley Sugar Shack	19
Hadley Night at the Hadley Historical Society	21
Founder's Day Celebration	22
Farm Tours: The UMass Hadley Farm	28
Golf Tournament	29
The Pride of Hadley Tulips	30
Farm Tours: Barstow's Dairy, The Hartsbrook School and Wancyzk Nursery	31
The Millicent H. Kauffman Award for Distinguished Service	34
Memorial Day Parade	35
Antique Tractor Show	38

Summer

Mt. Holyoke Hikes	44
Farm Tours: Hibbard Farm, Mapleline Farm and Astarte Farm	47
Hadley 350th Photo Exhibit Contest and Heritage Display	48
Riding Tour of West Street Common	50
Historical Society Open House	51
Hopkins Academy All Class Reunion	52
350th Parade	54
House Decorating Contest	64
July 4th Fireworks	66
Celebrating Hadley's APR Leadership	68
Hadley Art Exhibit in the Corn Barn of the Porter-Phelps-Huntington House	69
Garden and Artist Tour, Artist Festival	70

Farm Tours: Great Meadow Fruits, Hartsbrook Farm, Plainville Farm and Twin Oaks Farm	74
Eddie Forman Orchestra Polka Party	76
Girl Scout Outdoor Movie Night	78
Hadley Sampler: An Anniversary Celebration, 1659–2009	79
Block Party	81
Firemen's Muster	82
Farm Tours: Cook Farm's 100th, North Hadley Sugar Shack, and The Food Bank Farm	84

Autumn

Amherst 250th Parade	90
Reune with a Tune	91
350th "5K for Farmland" Road Race	92
The First Congregational Church of Hadley: Celebrating 350 Years of Worship and Service	93
Angels of Hadley Play	100
The History Fair	102
"350 x 24" Hadley Artists on Exhibit	108
New "Welcome to Hadley" Sign	110
Dedication of the Russell Plaques	111
Congratulatory Letters	112
Special Thank Yous	118
Sponsors	120
Volunteers	123
2009 Agricultural Map	126

Town of Hadley
350TH ANNIVERSARY COMMEMORATIVE BOOK

Looking north, West and Middle Streets

Mapleline Farm, Comins Road

North Hadley

Route 9 looking east

Looking south towards the Mt. Holyoke Range

HISTORY OF HADLEY

For thousands of years, people have been settling in this bend of the Connecticut River, drawn here by the rich soil, access to the water, and scenic vistas.

Once covered by a vast glacier that gave way in time to a large glacial lake (Lake Hitchcock), the Connecticut River Valley around 10,000 BC became home to Paleo-Indians who initiated centuries of human occupation. By the sixteenth century AD, the Valley sustained Algonkian peoples who hunted and fished here.

As early as 1614, the residents of the Valley began to encounter the first representatives of Euro-

Russell School in 1909 decorated for the 250th Celebration. (Photo courtesy of Ted McQueston)

pean nations exploring North America. In time, English colonists driven in part by a search for religious freedom began to settle the Connecticut Valley. A dissenting Connecticut congregation under the leadership of Rev. John Russell in 1659 founded Hadley as an agricultural community on the banks of the Connecticut River. John Pynchon purchased the site of the new settlement, a fertile peninsular plain defined by a bend in the Connecticut River, from the Nolwotogg community on behalf of those settlers. The first settlers laid out this area, formerly known as the Norwottuck Meadow, as the center of the new settlement before their arrival, with the Town Common, referred to as "the Broad Street," as the central feature. The common measured twenty rods wide and one mile long, with the Connecticut River defining both ends, and was reportedly based on the original plan of Wethersfield, Connecticut. Eight-acre home lots were ranged along both sides of the common, with farmlands behind.

In 1675–76, during King Philip's War, to guard against Indian attacks, a palisade that ran far enough behind the houses to include most of the barns and farm buildings enclosed the street and common. Legend has it that, during that conflict, the town was saved from destruction when, at a critical moment, William Goffe—one of the English judges who sentenced King Charles I to death, and was now hunted as a regicide—showed up in the midst of the townspeople, warned them of the danger, and led the town in fending off the assault, disappearing shortly afterward. Because in the story he appeared so miraculously, Goffe later became known as "The Angel of Hadley."

Through the years, the common remained the focus of town life. The meetinghouse occupied a prominent site, animals were pastured on the open land, militia drills were held periodically, and Hadley's Liberty Pole was erected there during the Revolutionary War. Taverns at the north and south ends and at the center of the common served the needs of passengers on the ferry, stagecoach, and riverboat routes.

As the number of settlers grew and they dispersed across the land, the desire for local places of worship also grew. As an answer to the problems of settlers traveling many miles to church, the communities of Hatfield, Granby, South Hadley and Amherst formed from the sprawling town of Hadley. The town continued to grow as an agricultural center. While farming was most common during this time, the exporting of everything from produce to beef to furs grew. Most of the products were taken by flatboat down the Connecticut River and overland to the Boston area as well. It was after 1792 that broomcorn became the dominant crop in Hadley. So abundant was this crop that Hadley would come to be known as the nation's broomcorn and broom manufacturing capital. Broom and brush making became a thriving industry here, exporting all across New York and New England, and as far as Ohio.

Over time the soil that produced so much broomcorn slowly depleted. By 1840, tobacco would take its place as the major crop as well as seed onions and other vegetables. The Massachusetts

Central Railroad crossed the northern half of the common in 1887, providing a faster way for Hadley farmers to ship their produce to market. The Connecticut Valley Street Railway, laid out along Russell Street about 1900, made local travel to Northampton and Amherst easier.

During these same years, the scenic quality of Hadley landscapes also began to draw attention. In the early nineteenth century, a painting of the "oxbow" by Thomas Cole—taken from the top of the Holyoke Range—made Hadley one of the most famous landscapes in the nation, and one of the first destinations to emerge in a burgeoning tourist industry.

It was during the late 1800s that, because of labor shortages and a drop in land values, Hadley experienced a decline in farming. It was also about this time that a large number of Irish, French Canadian and, later, Polish immigrants who were recruited from Ellis Island for labor purposes settled in Hadley. It was the Polish immigrants who are credited with saving Hadley's farmland as they worked the fine Hadley soil back into fertility. By 1920, asparagus became the popular crop in Hadley, soon making the town the asparagus capital of the world. Despite a disease that wiped out much of the crop in the 1950s, asparagus remains a hallmark of the community today.

Today, while commercial development has flourished in Hadley, the town remains largely agricultural and residential. Though malls and commercial businesses now lie along Russell Street on Route 9 to the east of the town's center, Hadley has the largest number of acres in agriculture in the Pioneer Valley, which includes crops of corn, potatoes, tobacco and scores of other vegetables. At the turn of the 21st century, Hadley is emerging as a leader in the preservation of those historic agricultural landscapes. The

---

2009 Hadley Statistics

Settled: 1659
Incorporated: 1661
Area: 24.75 Square Miles
Population (Town Census): 5178
Registered Voters: 3738
Tax Rate (Fiscal Year 2010): $9.32
Total Valuation (Fiscal Year 2010): $924,919,288
Form of Government: Open Town Meeting
Public Schools: Hopkins Academy and Hadley Elementary School
Town Highways: 66 Miles
State Highways: 9 Miles
Public Libraries: Goodwin Memorial Library, and North Hadley Library
Parks: Lion's Club Park, Town Common, and Skinner State Park
Service Clubs: Hadley Grange, Hadley Historical Society, Inc., Hadley Lions Club, Hadley Men's Club, Hadley Mothers' Club, Hadley PTO, Hadley Young Men's Club, Post 271 American Legion
Museums: Farm Museum, Historical Room in Goodwin Library, Porter-Phelps-Huntington House

1902 trolley filled with party goers. (Photo courtesy of the Hadley Historical Society)

Hockanum Rural Historic District was among the first efforts in Massachusetts to advance the National Park Service's aims to document rural districts. Community groups have partnered with state agencies to vigorously preserve the scenic assets of the Holyoke Range. A substantial amount of Hadley farmland has been preserved under the APR program, and significant effort has been made to document and preserve the Great Meadow, a unique landscape in the crook of the Connecticut River that may be the last extant example of open field agriculture in the United States—named in 2004 by PreservationMass, a statewide historic preservation group, one of the commonwealth's "Ten Most Endangered Historic Resources." In 2009, the World Monuments Fund included the "cultural landscape of Hadley, Mass." (specifically, the Great Meadow and Route 47) on its watch list of important landmarks to save around the world. The list included 93 sites in 47 countries. Hadley was one of only seven sites in the United States. Today, Hadley is a town that sees an exciting future deeply rooted in its rich heritage.

Back row left to right: Kristen Styspeck (inset), Gerry Devine, Chip Parsons, Mary Lou Laurenza, John Vassallo, David Martula, Sandi Buckhout, Wayne Buckhout. Front row left to right: Betty Fydenkevez, Mary Thayer, MaryAnn Mish, Joyce West

350th Committee Members

- Sandi Buckhout
- Wayne Buckhout
- Gerry Devine
- Betty Fydenkevez
- Mary Lou Laurenza
- David Martula, *Co-chair*
- Marla Miller
- MaryAnn Mish
- Chip Parsons
- Kristen Styspeck, *Secretary*
- Mary Thayer, *Co-chair*
- John Vassallo, *Treasurer*
- Joyce West

We thank these former members of the 350th Committee, who contributed so much during the beginning planning stages of the 350th Celebration:

Bill Banack, Harry Barstow, Michael Farnum, Ken Foley, Jo-Ann Konieczny, David Moskin, Tom Waskiewicz, and Debbie Windoloski.

INTRODUCTION

The year 2009 has been a truly memorable one for Hadley. The 350th Celebration began in January with a sparkling Snow and Ice Dinner Dance, and continued all year long. All of the ninety-plus events were successful and greatly enjoyed. It has been a year of community, appreciation, celebration, learning about our past, and experiencing the many facets of Hadley today.

In June 2004, the initial 350th Steering Committee was appointed by the Select Board with input from the Historical Commission. Nine of the original eighteen members remained on the committee through 2010. Over the years, four more members were added to this incredibly talented and hard working committee. A huge boost came to the Committee in May 2007, when the town voted $25,000 to fund the 350th anniversary. Not only was 20% of the estimated budget covered, but it showed there was a high level of interest and enthusiasm from the community. Soon after, three banks—Florence Savings Bank, Easthampton Savings Bank and Peoples Bank—stepped forward with major pledges. The 350th Committee knew its planning could now go ahead full speed. The support that it received from the business community, the residents, and town employees has been tremendous. The members of the 350th Committee were only one small part of Hadley's 350th Celebration. There were so many people who worked on subcommittees or assisted the 350th committee with their skills, talents and dedication. For example, the thirteen-member Parade Committee was formed shortly after the 350th Committee and they handled all aspects of the parade, enabling the 350th Committee to work on everything else. Other individuals and groups came forward with fully developed, and often fully funded, ideas, which added significantly to the celebration.

This book commemorates Hadley's 350th Celebration. It captures the spirit, community and fun felt at the various events during the year. The book is divided into seasons, and is in chronological order with a few exceptions. For the purposes of clarity and continuity, the Hadley Village Music Concert Series at the North Hadley Congregational Church is presented in a single section under "Winter," and the individual performances are listed on the 350th Anniversary Events page. The year long series of activities organized by the Hadley Historical Commission are also presented together in the "Winter" section.

Many of the descriptions of the events were submitted by their respective committee chairs, while the book's co-editors contributed material as well. The majority of photographs were taken by Rick Thayer, with some by Mary Thayer; photos taken by others are so noted.

It has been a privilege to serve Hadley on the 350th Committee. The committee members have learned so much more about this wonderful town, and met so many incredible people who call Hadley home.

—Mary Thayer, *Co-chair*
on behalf of the 350th Committee
March, 2010

350TH ANNIVERSARY EVENTS

January 24	Snow and Ice Dinner Dance
January 25	Concert: "Live the Dream: from King to Obama," with Evelyn Harris
February 8	Concert: "Sacred Harp Shape Note Community Sing"
February 15	Lecture: "WWI in Hadley" with Lisa West and Alice Nash
March 15	Lecture: "America's Blind Naturalist: Clarence Hawkes and the World He Lived In" with James A. Freeman
March 20	Girl Scout History Fair
March 28	Farm Tours: Montgomery Rose and North Hadley Sugar Shack
April 2	Float Building Workshop
April 4	Concert: "A Cappella Delight," with Lyra, High Definitions, Honest Harmony, The Quintessentials, The Dreamboats and 5-Alone
April 8	Hadley Night at the Hadley Historical Society
April 18	Founder's Day Celebration
April 18	Farm Tours: The UMass Hadley Farm
April 19	Lecture: "East Europeans Come to Hadley, Massachusetts"
May 2	Golf Tournament
May 2	Farm Tours: The UMass Hadley Farm: Sheep Shearing
May 3	Farm Tours: Barstow's Dairy, The Hartsbrook School and Wancyzk Nursery
May 7	The Millicent H. Kauffman Award for Distinguished Service
May 8	Nature Hike at Skinner State Park: "Flowers, Birds, and Trees, Oh My!"
May 17	Walking Tour of the Town Common with Kevin Sweeney
May 17	Concert: "It Hadley Be You" with the New Valley Singers
May 24	Memorial Day Parade
May 24	Antique Tractor Show
May 29	Nature Hike at Skinner State Park: "Hidden History Along the Auto Road"
May 31	North Hadley Congregational Church Galilean Service
June 6	Farm Tours: Hibbard Farm, Mapleline Farm and Astarte Farm
June 7	Opening Reception for the Photo Contest at the Summit House on Mt. Holyoke
June 7	Concert: "Native American Flutes," with Barry White Crow Higgins
June 11	Walking Tour: "Evidence for the Early Defensive Fortifications of Hadley" with Ed Hood
June 13	Riding Tour of West Street Common
June 13	Historical Society Open House
June 13	Open House at Hopkins Academy
June 13	Hopkins Academy All Class Reunion
June 14	350th Parade
June 14	Post Parade Party at the Young Men's Club
June 27	Farm Tours: Lakeside U-Pick Strawberries
June 28	Nature Hike at Skinner State Park: "Fire, Ice and Rocks on the Range"

July 4	July 4th Fireworks
July 5	Hadley Art Exhibit Reception, Porter-Phelps-Huntington House Corn Barn
July 7	Celebrating Hadley's APR Leadership
July 16	Lecture: "The Clockworks at the First Church," with John Nelson
July 18	Garden and Artist Tour, Artist Festival
July 26	Farm Tours: Great Meadow Fruits, Hartsbrook Farm, Plainville Farm, and Twin Oaks Farm
August 8	Eddie Forman Orchestra Polka Party
August 14	Girl Scout Outdoor Movie Night
August 22	Chicken BBQ & Corn Fest with the Music of Rani Arbo & daisy mayhem
August 22	Hadley Sampler: An Anniversary Celebration, 1659–2009
September 12	Firemen's Muster
September 12	Block Party
September 13	Concert: "Ed Rosser, Piano"
September 20	Farm Tours: Cook Farm's 100th, North Hadley Sugar Shack
September 21	Farm Tours: The Food Bank Farm
September 26	Craft Fair and Music Fest at North Hadley Church
September 27	Amherst 250th Parade
October 4	Concert: Allan Taylor, on the organ
October 9	Concert: "Reune with a Tune"
October 18	350th "5K for Farmland" Road Race
October 18	The First Congregational Church of Hadley: Celebrating 350 Years of Worship and Service
October 18	Lecture: "Half-hanged Mary: Mary Webster and Witchcraft in Early Hadley" with Bridget Marshall and Brian Ogilvie
October 23	*Angels of Hadley* Play, repeated October 24 and 25
October 24	Hadley History Day
October 24	Open House at the Historical Society Museum
October 24	Fall Harvest Supper at the First Congregational Church
October 25	Coffee Hour and Displays at the Most Holy Redeemer Church
October 25	Book Signing by Authors of *Cultivating a Past: Essays on the History of Hadley*
October 25	Concert: "Songs of Inspiration"
November 7	Opening Reception for "350x24" Hadley Artists on Exhibit at the U.S. Fish & Wildlife Service
November 15	Concert: "Stephen Katz, Cello"
November 15	Lectures "Before Hadley: Archaeology and Native History, 10,000 BC–1700 AD" with Siobhan Hart, and "Quanquan's Mortgage of 1663" with Alice Nash
December 5	Holiday Sing-a-long
December 6	Lecture: "The Hadley Barn Survey," with Bonnie Parsons, Pioneer Valley Planning Commission

WINTER

Opposite page: View of the Devine Farm from Comins Road; cupola on barn in North Hadley. Clockwise from top left: Tractor in North Hadley; doorway on West Street; doorway on East Street.

SNOW AND ICE DINNER DANCE

The night was clear and cold. The temperature outside was in the low teens, but to the folks gathered at the Student Union Ballroom at the University of Massachusetts it made little difference. The valiant crowd had braved the weather to celebrate the Kick-off event of Hadley's 350th anniversary year, appropriately named, "Snow and Ice."

Snowflakes, snow-covered trees and candlelight festooned the room, providing the feeling of a winter wonderland. Master of Ceremonies Gerry Devine welcomed guests and spoke movingly of Hadley's proud heritage. A delicious dinner was served and enjoyed by everyone. U.S. Representative Richard Neal offered his sincere congratulations. State Senator Stanley Rosenberg and State Representative John Scibak presented the town with framed copies of early Hadley documents, papers they had preserved, in honor of Hadley's 350th. The music of Jeff Holmes and his band invited people to the dance floor, and the invitation was enthusiastically accepted by the joyful crowd. The evening flowed superbly to become a part of the history of Hadley that we were all celebrating. It will long be remembered as a delightful evening of festivity and merriment.

Above: The table centerpieces even had chocolate asparagus spears on top of the cakes.

Above: State Senator Stanley Rosenberg (at left) and State Representative John Scibak (at right) present a gift of preserved early Hadley documents to the Hadley Select Board, left to right: Brian West, Gerry Devine, Joyce Chunglo and Dan Dudkiewicz. Right: U.S. Representative Richard Neal congratulates Hadley's residents.

Above: Guests enjoyed dancing and delicious food. A slide show of historic Hadley photos was shown on the screen. Right: Gerry Devine gives a toast. Below: A table ready for guests.

Toast Given at the Snow and Ice Dinner Dance by Master of Ceremonies, Selectman Gerry Devine

Let us toast the 59 founding families whose conviction and brave spirit brought them, in 1659, to the wilderness soon to be known as Hadley.

Let us toast to our forefathers who built our great town with their hearts and hands and their souls.

Let us toast to ourselves to remind us to preserve our traditions and pass along a town rich in opportunities for those yet to come.

Let us toast to the future which will have the great wisdom of 350 years of history to grow on.

HADLEY VILLAGE MUSIC CONCERT SERIES

Hadley Village Music, led by Polly Keener, organized a year-long series of wonderful concerts, showcasing many local, very skilled, musicians. The North Hadley Congregational Church has amazing acoustics and was an ideal location for the concerts. The hospitality of the Church members was evident at each performance. The concerts added so much to the 350th celebration.

Above: High Definition, a vocal ensemble of the Northampton Community Music Center, and at right, 5-Alone from the Pioneer Valley Performing Arts Charter School, delight the audience.

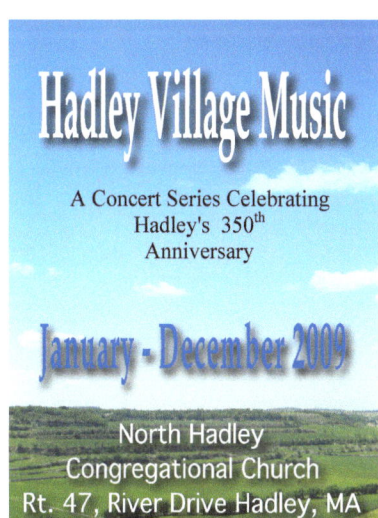

Top: Rani Arbo & daisy mayhem perform.
Right: Music lessons during intermission.

THE SOUVENIR SHOPPE

A corner room on the first floor of the Town Hall was transformed into the "Souvenir Shoppe" that was open to the public two to three days a week for a year and a half, thanks to a large, energetic, and enthusiastic group of volunteers.

The Souvenir Committee consisted of a core group that researched and selected what they hoped would become special mementos of this historic year. Some of the items selected included pottery from a Massachusetts potter, Christmas ornaments hand painted and numbered by a New York artist, note cards by Sandra Pipczynski, a Hadley photographer, and postcards that featured a mural painted by John Gnatek, a local artist. But the most popular item was the yellow "Grown in Hadley" asparagus t-shirts, worn by the young and the young-at-heart.

Throughout the year-long celebration, souvenirs were also set up and sold at the many events, as well as shipped out to those who saw the pictures on the 350th web site. The success of the souvenir committee was due to the combination of dedicated volunteers and great support from the community. Because of this commitment, not only did the products sell well and help contribute to the fundraising, but friendships were formed, ideas were shared, event information was readily available and all of those involved took great pride in being a a part of this very special year. Hopefully these mementos, as well as memories, will be treasured for years and generations to come.

Opposite page: Carter, Mary and Nolan Styspeck show off the Grown in Hadley t-shirts. (Photo by Sandi Buckhout) Top: The 350th Souvenir Committee: Wayne Buckhout, Sandi Buckhout, Andrea Goguen, Elaine Tudryn, Sarah Wanczyk and Joanne Keller. (Photo courtesy of Sandi Buckhout) Above: The Souvenir Shoppe in Town Hall.

A sample of the Hadley 350th souvenirs.

Above: Wayne and Sandi Buckhout on parade day. (Photo by Gerry Delisle) Below: Joyce West and Wayne Buckhout sell 350th souvenirs at the Antique Tractor Show.

PUBLICATIONS

Like the Souvenir Committee, before the anniversary year even commenced, the Publications Committee got busy assembling a calendar to promote the year's events. The beautifully-illustrated 2009 calendar was sponsored by Florence Savings Bank, The Hadley Garden Center, Esselon Café, North Hadley Sugar Shack, Cowl's Lumber, and Hadley at Elaine Care and Rehabilitation, and produced by The Benjamin Company.

Even before that—in fact, well before—work began on a volume of essays to celebrate the town's anniversary. Drawing on funds set aside several years ago by the Hadley Historical Commission to produce a supplement to Sylvester Judd's *History of Hadley* (which narrates Hadley's story only into the 18th century), planning began for an edited collection of essays modeled after the wonderful book that Northampton published for their own 350th celebration. With the balance of the funds needed generously donated by the late select board member Kate Nugent, the University of Massachusetts Press agreed to bring out the book titled *Cultivating a Past: Essays on the History of Hadley, Massachusetts*, a gathering of both published and unpublished essays on topics in the town's history from 10,000 BC to the present. The volume appeared in April 2009.

Once the work toward this hardcover, scholarly book was completed, committee members turned their attention to the development of a series of smaller paperback volumes on an array of topics sure to be of interest to Hadley residents. Everyone was delighted when Tom Pelissier agreed to donate his research on Hadley's French-Canadian community; Tom self-produced a beautifully illustrated pamphlet that represents the only research to date on this important subject. Meanwhile, working with White River Press and UMass graphic designer Patricia Nobre, work commenced on the booklet series, which also drew on local scholars and scholarship. Eric Freeman contributed a revised version of his paper on Hadley men in the Civil War, and James Freeman offered his research on the Angel of Hadley. The Hadley Historical Commission contributed a revised version of the historic resource study undertaken in recent years by a team of scholars at the University of Massachusetts, which will appear as *The Pride of All the Citizens: The West Street Common and Great Meadow in Hadley, Massachusetts*. The Historical Commission also generated new scholarship toward the cause, working with graduate students in the Public History Program at UMass to produce a history of the town's five cemeteries, and editing for publication a series of oral histories on farming in Hadley that have been collected under the Commission's auspices in recent years.

Three other publications of the 350th celebration are a Parade Photo Book with 106 pages and over 300 photos, covering all units of the parade, an *Angels of Hadley* photo book with 66 pages showing photos of the play, and this Commemorative volume before you.

As the anniversary year drew to a close the Hadley Historical Commission agreed to take on the ongoing oversight of these and future publications, work that will be on hand for future generations to enjoy.

Publications of Hadley's 350th celebration.

HADLEY HISTORICAL COMMISSION ACTIVITIES

Hadley's Historical Commission members were delighted to contribute to the celebration of the town's 350th. In order to advance its ongoing mission to document and preserve Hadley's historic buildings and landscapes, the Commission undertook—with funding from the Community Preservation Act—a large survey of barns and outbuildings. A monthly lecture series brought many local authors to speak about their work, and introduced Hadley residents to some other historians as well.

The year got off to a wintry start, and the first event in the lecture series, "Researching Your House," was snowed out, but the survey of Hadley barns and outbuildings was launched in January, as two bus tours traveled around town—in essence traveling oral history projects in which area farmers riding on a school bus driven by Duff Pipczynski regaled Commission members and survey consultant Bonnie Parsons with stories about the building and uses of area barns.

In February, the lecture series got off to its official start when Alice Nash and Lisa West presented two papers on WWI in Hadley. A packed house gathered at the Howard Johnson Inn to learn about the home front during the Great War, and the Influenza epidemic. In March, James Freeman spoke to another crowded house on "America's Blind Naturalist," Clarence Hawkes, a topic especially welcome among those residents who still remembered Mr. Hawkes. Jim's research also led to the declaration by the Massachusetts legislature of Clarence Hawkes day on October 24th, during the History Fair.

In April, the Hadley Senior Center filled to hear a panel of speakers covering a range of topics associated with the history of East Europeans in Hadley. John Skibiski and author and historian Stephen Jendrysik addressed broader patterns in the history of immigration, while Sonia Waskiewicz Chapnick, Stanley Fil, Joseph Pelis and Frank Zalot, Jr. shared more personal family histories. Stan Radosz, Director of the Polish Center of Discovery and Learning, gave an illustrated presentation. A particular highlight was the large exhibit of family memorabilia displayed by a number of attendees.

As spring arrived, the lecture series hit the road and walked Hadley's historic town common. On a rainy day in May, Amherst College professor Kevin Sweeney led a hardy group of residents on a tour that traced the architectural history of West Street, and in June, archaeologist Ed Hood led a second walking tour to search for "Evidence for the Early Defensive Fortifications of Hadley, Massachusetts." In July, the commissioners were all excited to unveil their float at the parade, and then they sat back to enjoy John Nelson as he presented a talk on "The Clockworks at the First

---

HADLEY HISTORICAL COMMISSION

Claire Carlson
Marla Miller
Margaret Freeman
Margaret Tudryn
Mitzi Sawada
Tom McGee
Meghan Gelardi Holmes
Brett Johnson
Ginger Goldsbury

Above, clockwise from left: Clockworks of the First Congregational Church; book signing for Cultivating A Past; bus tour of Hadley barns with area farmers. (Photo courtesy of the Hadley Historical Commission) Below: Ed Hood talks about Hadley's early fortifications.

 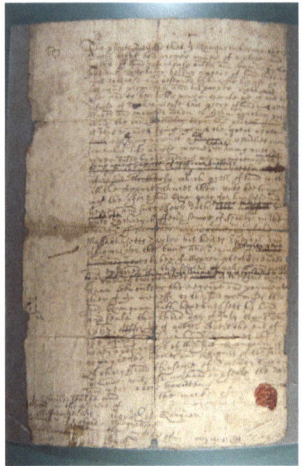 

Above left: Joe Pelis speaks about growing up in Hadley. Above center: The Quanquan Mortgage, one of Hadley's original documents, discussed by Alice Nash. Above right: John Nelson speaks about the clockworks at the First Church.

Church." The talk was given in the hall of the First Congregational Church, and guests were invited to walk up and see the clockworks.

In October, attention turned, appropriately enough, to witchcraft. UMass Amherst professor Brian Ogilvie and UMass Lowell professor Bridget Marshall teamed up to bring an enthusiastic audience up to date on the history of witchcraft in early modern Europe and Britain's North American colonies, and also on Hadley's most significant witchcraft episode, the story of "half-hanged Mary," or Mary Webster. Looking ahead toward holiday shopping, the Commission was pleased that same month when Hadley's Barnes and Nobles store organized an event to celebrate the publication of *Cultivating a Past.* The book's editor, Marla Miller, as well as authors Elizabeth Chilton, Lynne Bassett, Alice Nash, Jim Freeman, Bridget Marshall, Brian Ogilvie, and Ed Hood were on hand to sign copies and answer questions about their essays.

In November, UMass Anthropology Ph.D. Siobhan Hart and History professor Alice Nash teamed up to discuss Hadley's Native American past. Ms. Hart presented "Before Hadley: Archaeology and Native History, 10,000 BC–1700 AD," a paper based in part on work the Anthropology Department did to help the Hadley Historical Society steward its archaeological collections, while Alice Nash spoke on "Quanquan's Mortgage of 1663," a locally-iconic document that sheds light on the arrival of Europeans on the land that would become Hadley.

The year ended with a lively talk by Bonnie Parsons of the Pioneer Valley Planning Commission, who summarized the results of the Barn Survey funded by the CPA program. The program was illustrated with beautiful images of the barns of Hadley, part of the agricultural and architectural heritage of the town's history that the Commission is working to preserve. Over the course of the 350th year the commission also worked to bring out a history of the town common, a history of the five town cemeteries, and an edited collection of some of the oral histories that they've been gathering in recent years. The commissioners are excited to be collaborating with the 350th Publications Committee to see those works in print in the coming year, and hope to continue the excitement that the 350th generated as the town enters its next half century.

HOPKINS ACADEMY

As Hopkins Academy Principal Diana Bonneville explained on the school's website, the school focused on an interdisciplinary unit throughout the school year. Each teacher incorporated Hadley's 350th anniversary and/or immigration into his or her curriculum. Some of these units included: Polish and Irish immigration in the 19th century, statistical analysis relative to immigrant population, Route 9 traffic studies, post and beam architecture, a quilt celebrating Hadley's history, historical perspectives on food and fashion in the region, historical literature, and an analysis of the Connecticut River. Student Council President Kate Brewer worked on an independent study examining various aspects of Hadley's history. She organized student assemblies that highlighted the upcoming celebratory events, such as the *Angels of Hadley* play and the June parade. Mary Thayer, co-chairperson of Hadley's 350th committee, and Jeffrey Dreisbach, representing the *Angels of Hadley* play, spoke to the students and encouraged their active participation in these memorable events. Later on in the year, the art students with guidance from their art teacher Marilyn Judah, designed and made a float representing the Hadley Public Schools for the 350th parade.

Top: Hopkins Academy students work on the nest for the 350th float. Above: Hopkins Academy students paint a sign for the float. They are, left to right, Mackenzie Babb, Emma Konieczny, Libby Kielb, Marilyn Judah (art teacher), Jessica Stowell, Rachel Walsh, and Nick Devine. (Photos courtesy of Marilyn Judah)

SPRING

GIRL SCOUT HISTORY FAIR

In March, the Hopkins cafeteria was filled with historical displays by local girl scouts from Hadley and Amherst. About 120 girls from eleven troops researched various aspects of the area's history to mark the 350th anniversary in Hadley and the 250th anniversary in Amherst. Display topics included broom corn and broom making, the wonderful local soil, toys through the years, and more.

Above: Hopkins Academy middle school girl scouts stand in front of their display of "Farming in Hadley" at the Girl Scout Fair. The girls are (left to right) Katelyn Szczepanski, Kayla Jacque, Karoline Moriarty, Sarah Thelen. Below: Claire Callahan is sharing this Hadley Broom Making display as part of her Girl Scout Silver Project with troop member Holly Czjakowski (left).

FARM TOURS: MONTGOMERY ROSE AND NORTH HADLEY SUGAR SHACK

In March we had the first of a series of farm tours organized by members of the farming community, led by Beth Cook and Paula Barstow. (The map used for the farm tours is at the back of this book.) It was a real treat to see inside the farm operations throughout the growing season; the hundreds of people who turned out for these events learned a lot about agriculture in Hadley. Walking through the farm fields was another way to connect with Hadley's farming past and traditions.

The tours started with Montgomery Rose (montgomeryrose.com). Montgomery Rose was founded in 1909 by Alexander Montgomery. He developed the award winning "Hadley Rose." In 1959 the company was purchased by the Johnson family, which owns it today. The tour brought the visitors through the greenhouses, where they were shown how the lilies, gerbera daisies, gardenias and stephanotis are grown, stored and packaged. The soil composting operation is an important part of the process. Seeing the greenhouses full of beautiful flowers in March was a treat, and each visitor left with an immense bouquet of lilies.

Above: Gerbera daisies at Montgomery Rose. Top: Lilies.

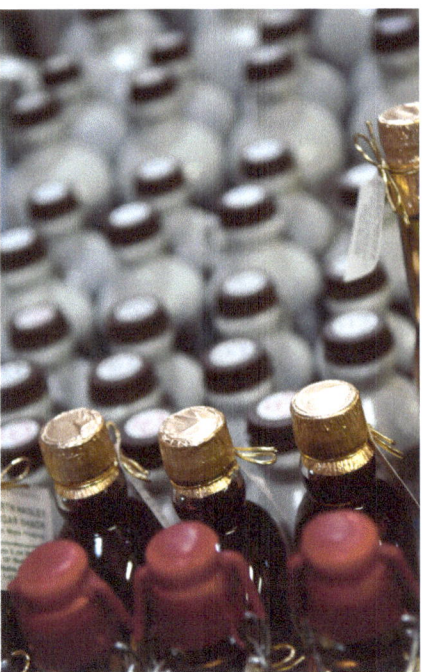

Above, clockwise from left: John Boisvert boils maple sap into syrup; steam venting from the roof is a sure sign the maple syrup is being boiled; jugs of maple syrup are ready for purchase.

The next stop that day was the North Hadley Sugar Shack at Boisvert Farm (northhadley sugarshack.com). The Sugar Shack is the name of the sugarhouse/farm stand built during 1995 by John and Joe Boisvert. In early fall through the month of December, the farm stand sells produce from the farm: pumpkins, squash, garlic, onions, potatoes along with many maple products. The annual display of mums and asters is beautiful. But the spring tour focused on sugaring. Maple syrup is produced here in early spring and crowds turn out every year for breakfast. Farm tour visitors got to see the maple syrup being made, as well as the building where the syrup is bottled and made into candies. The aroma of the maple sap being boiled and the sight of the steam rising from the roof vent were welcome signs of spring. The sweet taste of the warm maple syrup was delicious.

HADLEY NIGHT AT THE HADLEY HISTORICAL SOCIETY

The Hadley Historical Society, which exists to promote interest in and an understanding of Hadley's great heritage, was honored to have been a part of the town's 350th Anniversary Celebration in 2009. On April 8, 2009, the society asked residents and friends to share their Hadley photos, items of interest, stories and experiences. Mary and Rick Thayer added to the evening with their beautiful display showcasing the upcoming events for this grand celebration, that demonstrated Hadley as the ultimate hometown.

The Hadley Historical Society in honor of the 350th donated three handmade copper lanterns that were affixed to the front entrance of the Town Hall as a memorial to Dorothy Russell, the town's historian, and a founder of the Historical Society.

The lanterns on the Town Hall were donated by the Hadley Historical Society.

FOUNDER'S DAY CELEBRATION

The April 18th Founder's Day event began on the town common. Descendants from 33 of the town's founding families came from near and far (Florida, Ohio, Washington, DC). Descendants wore name tags listing their name, and the name(s) of the founding family/families they came from. Some were descended from eleven, twelve or thirteen of the founders!

The people gathered on the town common introduced themselves to their very distant cousins, compared genealogical information, and exchanged email addresses. Everyone then processed down Route 9 to the Town Hall. At the head of the procession was the Polish American Veteran's Drum Corps, followed by a horse-drawn wagon from Barry Robert's Muddy Brook Farm. Those who weren't riding in the wagon walked behind, down Russell Street. At the town hall, Rev. Sarah Buteux of the First Congregational Church led the group in prayer. Mary Thayer and David Martula, co-chairs of the 350th Committee, welcomed the group and Marla Miller, Co-Chair of the Hadley Historical Commission, spoke, followed by Select Board members Gerry Devine (a member of the Hadley 350th Committee and the organizer of the Founder's Day event) and Joyce Chunglo. Senator Stanley Rosenberg and Representative John Scibak rededicated their gift of founding papers to the town. At the Church, a beautiful Founder's Day cake was cut by the oldest resident in town, Victoria Drabek. There were some displays and a historical slide show on view in the church. The Farm Museum, the Library, the Historical Museum room upstairs above the town library, and the Souvenir Shoppe in town hall were open for the afternoon.

Prayer given by the Rev. Sarah Buteux

The Rev. Sarah Buteux opens with a prayer.

Dear Lord, God of our mothers and our fathers, in this time of remembrance we come, as have the generations before us, to seek your blessing and to speak your praise. For the richness of this land we call Hadley, for good soil and clean water, for the blessing of sun and shade, mountain and valley, we give you thanks.

We give thanks to you gracious God, for those who built this community from the ground up with their faith and labor and for those who sustain it even now with their loyalty and trust. For those who cleared the fields round us with vision and for those who sow these fields even now with hope, we give you praise. For those who laid the foundations of our churches and our schools, our Town Hall and our library, for those who carry on the work of their ancestors tilling fields and raising stock, and for those who work day in and day out in this community to protect and serve, educate and build, nourish and heal, we ask your blessing.

Come now Sovereign Lord and walk amongst us. Keep our celebrations honest as we recall the past, compassionate as we judge the present, and hopeful as we engage the future.

And may we be mindful, O Lord, of all our blessings; for you have taught us that you will require much from those to whom much is given. Grant that we whom you have called to see so good and Godly a heritage, may extend more abundantly to others what we so richly enjoy here in Hadley, that in serving others we may come to know the glory of serving you. Amen and Amen.

Opposite page: The Founder's Day procession goes from the Town Common to the Town Hall. Top: Descendants of Hadley's founding families sign in. Middle: the Founder's Day cake. Above: Miriam Pratt enjoys the festivities.

Welcome given by Mary Thayer, co-chair of the Hadley 350th Committee

Mary Thayer welcomes the Founder's Day Crowd.

Welcome to Hadley's Founder's Day, as we look back to April 18, 1659, when 59 men committed to leave their established homes in Hartford, Wethersfield and Windsor, and move with their families to the wilds of Massachusetts. Today we are grateful to these leaders in their communities for their courage and moral conviction.

We try to imagine what it was like 350 years ago. The only communities in Western Massachusetts at that time were Springfield, settled in 1636 and the trading village of Northampton, settled in 1654. We try to imagine the settlers' hardships and daily life. And we honor their many descendants who are with us today. It is fitting that our celebration today is on the Town Common, which was first laid out in the 1660s, and at the Town Hall and the First Congregational Church, the founding church of the town.

Also, welcome to Hadley's ongoing 350th celebration. Throughout this year we are celebrating Hadley's past and present, and looking into its future. Through the Historical Commission's lecture series, the events of the Historical Society, our website, hadley350.org and through other 350th events, we are learning about life in Hadley throughout these years.

We learn about the people here before the Europeans came. We learn about life in the 1600s, when all the houses were on West Street. Then we learn about the expansion in the 1720s, as people felt safe to venture outside the protection of the palisades, or fence, around the homes on the street. These children and grandchildren of the original settlers, as well as newcomers from Connecticut, Eastern Massachusetts and other places, ventured east, north and south, still within Hadley. As the population grew in these areas, and a minister of their own could be supported, the hardship of getting to Hadley's meetinghouse for worship led to precincts being formed. Some of these precincts grew into towns. Hatfield had broken off first in 1670, as the difficulty of crossing the Connecticut River in harsh weather was too great a barrier. South Hadley was incorporated in 1753 and Amherst in 1759.

From Hadley's 80 square miles in the 1660s, to its 25 square miles now, the towns of Hatfield, South Hadley, Amherst, Granby, Whately, parts of Williamsburg, Belchertown and Sunderland have sprung. Hadley's celebration of its founding today is also a celebration of the beginnings of these neighboring towns. We welcome the representatives of these towns here with us today.

We learn about life in the 1800s, with the shift of the center of town to Back Street, where we stand now. We learn about the Irish and French Canadian immigrants, and then the Eastern European immigrants towards the end of the century, about the industry and mills in town, and the advent of the railroad.

We learn about life in the 1900s, with the huge transformation in technology, from the advent of the automobile, electricity and trucking, the effects of the growth of UMass, to the huge expansion of business, to life as we know it today.

In each century, Hadley has remained an agricultural town, has met the challenges of daily life, and has answered calls for war. Other people from across our country, from Asia and other places in the world, have joined the town, too. Throughout its 350 years, Hadley has maintained its character, its community and its pride, that began with the Founders.

So please join us as we celebrate this year, we have many events ahead, there is something for everyone. Together we are making this year a truly memorable one.

Welcome given by Marla Miller, co-chair of the Hadley Historical Society and member of the Hadley 350th Committee

Marla Miller addresses the Founder's Day crowd.

Founder's Day: As co-chair of the Hadley Historical Commission, it is my pleasure to add yet another welcome to today's festivities, part of a wonderful, year-long celebration of Hadley's history.

When Gerry Devine first asked me if I would say a few words to help mark this occasion, I could hardly think where to begin. When I first became interested in Hadley's history, some twenty years ago now, I was particularly interested in the Revolutionary generations—the women and men whose labor in the late eighteenth and early nineteenth centuries helped transform Massachusetts from colony to Commonwealth. Today our focus is drawn still further backward in time, to the first of the English families who found this spot on a bend in the Connecticut River an appealing place to search for faith and fortune in the New World. The documents that will be rededicated today speak powerfully of that generation of migrants looking for a place to call home, just as the Nonotuck people who preceded them, and many other generations of migrants have done in the decades since.

As a historian, I always find documents like these incredibly moving. They remind us of the dedication and energy of other people at other times, and along the way can't help but inspire us to be dedicated and energetic in our own time. Seeing them today underscores for me how important it is to preserve the artifacts of those stories, from documents like these to the buildings like this beautiful Town Hall, and landscapes like the spectacular Common we've come from today. I hope you'll take some time today to go into the Farm Museum, or the Library and the Hadley Historical Society room upstairs, and pause to appreciate not just the men and women who founded our community, but also the men and women who had the foresight to preserve the documents and artifacts gathered there, the things that afford us these precious glimpses into our town's past.

And more than that, I hope that these festivities will cause you to give some thought, too, to your own family's contributions to our Town and its history, and help us preserve more of that story for our own descendents, the people who are going to gather on these very same steps a hundred years from now and wonder what life was like in the 1950s as well as the 1650s, who will continue to wonder about the 17th century founders, as well as their many generations of descendents, and the people who came along later to found other important things, from new communities and neighborhoods to new civic and social organizations to new business enterprises.

Put another way, one great way to honor our founders is to keep preserving the history they helped launch. Ever since I came to Hadley some years ago, I've been impressed by the dedication and energy of its citizens on behalf of its history. When I first moved here, it was the tireless efforts of Dorothy Russell that first struck me as remarkable. Since that time I've had occasion to witness first-hand how hard people have worked here to preserve Hadley's legacy, from the Town Hall Exterior Committee—the first committee I had the privilege to serve on in town—to the Hadley Historical Commission, the Cemetery Commission, the Historical Society, the Town Clerk and Library Trustees, the hardworking members of the 350th steering committee, and the ad hoc community of farm families who have organized a steady series of events to celebrate our agricultural heritage. As we honor Hadley's long history, let's honor too the many people who have, though the years, contributed to making it, and to preserving it as well.

Hadley Founding Families

"At a meeting at Goodman Ward's house, in Hartford, April 18th, 1659, the company there met engaged themselves under their own hands, or by their deputies, whom they had chosen, to remove themselves and their families out of the jurisdiction of Connecticut into the jurisdiction of the Massachusetts, as may appear in a paper dated the day and year abovesaid. Then names of the engagers are these:" (59 signed the document, *18 of them did not move or stayed just a short time). Information on these pages is from Sylvester Judd, *History of Hadley* (Springfield, Mass: H. R. Huntting & Company, 1905) pp. 11–31.

From Hartford

John Webster
William Goodwin
John Crow
Nathaniel Ward
John White
John Barnaard
Andrew Bacon
William Lewis
William Westwood
Richard Goodman
John Arnold*
William Partrigg
Gregory Wilterton*
Thomas Standley
Richard Church
Ozias Goodwin*
Francis Barnard
James Ensign*
George Steele*
John Marsh
Robert Webster*
William Lewis, Jr.*
Nathaniel Standley
Samuel Church
William Markum
Samuel Moody
Zechariah Field
Widow Westly*
Widow Watson*
Andrew Warner
Richard Billings
Benj. Harbert*
Edward Benton*
John Catling*
Mr. Samuel Hooker*
Capt. John Cullick*
 (not fully engaged)
Daniel Warner

From Wethersfield

Mr. John Russell Junior
Nathaniel Dickinson
Samuel Smith
Thomas Coleman
John Russell, senior
John Dickinson
Philip Smith
John Coleman
Thomas Wells
James Northam
Samuel Gardner
Thomas Edwards*
John Hubbard
Thomas Dickinson
Robert Boltwood
Samuel Smith, Jr.*
William Gull
Luke Hitchcock*
Richard Montague
John Latimer*

From Windsor

Samuel Porter
Peter Tilton
John Hawkes

Hadley's Early Settlement

Owners of Houselots in the Village on the East Side of the River in 1663

Samuel Gardner
Chileab Smith
Joseph Baldwin
Robert Boltwood
Francis Barnard
John Hawks
Richard Church
Edward Church
Samuel Church
Henry Clark
Stephen Terry
Andrew Warner
John Marsh
Timothy Nash
John Webster
William Goodwin
John Crow
Samuel Moody
Nathaniel Wood
William Markham
Joseph Kellogg
A. Nichols
John Ingram
John Taylor
William Pixley
William Partrigg
Thomas Coleman
Samuel Smith
Philip Smith
Richard Montague
John Dickinson
Samuel Porter
Thomas Wells
John Hubbard
Mr. John Russell, Jr.
John Barnard
Andrew Bacon
Nathaniel Stanley
Thomas Stanley
John White
Peter Tilton

The Polish American Veteran's Drum Corps leads the Founder's Day procession down Russell Street.

William Lewis
Richard Goodman
William Westwood
Aaron Cooke
Thomas Dickinson
Nathaniel Dickinson
John Russell, Sr.

Owners of Houselots in the Village on the West Side of the River in 1668

William King
Samuel Field
Benjamin Wait
John Graves, Jr.
Samuel Foote
Robert Danks

Isaac Graves, JR
Samuel Northam
Richard Morton
John Hawks
Samuel Kellogg
Obadiah Dickinson
John Allis
Daniel White
William Allis
Thomas Meekins
Thomas Meekins, Jr.
Eleazar Frary
John Graves
Isaac Graves
Stephen Taylor
Barnabas Hinsdale

Ozias Goodwin
Mr. Hope Atherton
Zechariah Field
John Field
John Cowles
John Cowles, Jr.
Richard Fellows
Widow Fellows
Thomas Bracy
Hezekiah Dickinson
William Scott
Daniel Belden
Samuel Allis
Samuel Marsh
Nathaniel Foote
Philip Russell
Samuel Gillet

John Wells
John Coleman
Samuel Belden
William Gull
Samuel Dickinson
Edward Benton
Nathaniel
  Dickinson, Sr.
John White, Jr.
Nicholas Worthington
Nathaniel
  Dickinson, Jr.
Richard Billing
Samuel Billing
Daniel Warner
Thomas Bull

SPRING 27

FARM TOURS: THE UMASS HADLEY FARM

The University of Massachusetts Hadley Farm (umass.edu/vasci) had several tours. The Hadley Farm is one of the teaching farms for the department of Veterinary and Animal Sciences at the University of Massachusetts Amherst. They feature Dorset sheep, Boer, goats, alpacas, Belted Galloways and horses, sell breeding stock, meat and wool products, and have a community riding program. The farm was open again on May 2nd and 3rd for a sheep shearing demonstration.

Top: Pig pile at the UMass farm. Above: What are ewe looking at?

GOLF TOURNAMENT

Ken Rodak organized a Golf Tournament, held on May 2nd, to raise funds for the Firemen's Muster and Block Party. The tournament was at the Southampton Country Club, and 28 golfers participated. The winning team of Kevin Rodak, Pat Lemieux, Ken Rodak and Johnaton Sicard shot a round of (−12). The participants enjoyed a steak dinner after the tournament.

Above: Winning golf team: Ken Rodak, Pat Lemieux, Kevin Rodak, Johnaton Sicard. Left: Ron Blajda and Dave Hahn enjoy the golf tournament. (Photos courtesy of Ken Rodak)

THE "PRIDE OF HADLEY" TULIPS

In April, thousands of the red tulips were seen all over town, a beautiful welcome to spring and our 350th events to come. The Hopkins Academy Student Council and the Hadley Girl Scouts, in the fall of 2008, planted 1500 "Pride of Hadley" tulip bulbs on town property, to be enjoyed for years to come. Many residents and businesses also planted the tulips, extending the display throughout town.

Bags of tulips were purchased and donated to the town in memory or honor of someone special. Thank you to the following donors:

In memory of Alfred Torrielli by Andrea Goguen

In memory of the Hea Fey and Chunglo families by Joyce Chunglo

In memory of Victor Buckowski by Josh, Mary, Erin, and Braeden Tudryn

In memory of Martin and Mary Gowdey by Jean Gowdey

In memory of Sophie and Anthony Fydenkevez by Richard and Elizabeth Fydenkevez

In memory of Waldo and Marion Kendall by Wayne and Sandi Buckhout

In memory of Florence Thayer by Rick, Mary, Dan and Doug Thayer

In memory of Michael and Ann Casey by Cathleen F. Smith

In memory of Ken Lynch by Chris and Morgan Lynch

In memory of Thomas and Sally Fydenkevez by Gary, Brenda and Meghan Fydenkevez

In memory of Lucille Sienkiewicz by Paul and Marie Appleby

In memory of Frank Scott and his son, Fred Scott by Carolyn Hayes and family

In memory of Louis and Jessie (Scott) Agassiz by Carolyn Hayes and family

In memory of David A. Hayes by Carolyn Hayes and family

In memory of Walter & Marie Kopec by their family

In memory of Wayne Kopec by his family

In memory of Donald Shipman by Marjorie Barstow

In memory of Marion Purdy by Marjorie Barstow

In memory of Nelson Barstow by Marjorie Barstow

In memory of Richard Waskiewicz and Janet Keller by Joanne & Doug Keller and Matt, Brian & Carolyn Waskiewicz

In memory of the Kellogg family by Scott, Barbara and Tiffany Kellogg

In memory of William Kimbrel and Muggie by Elizabeth Lloyd-Kimbrel

In memory of their Nana, Diane Hengehold by Hadley and Hank Twichell

In honor of the Hadley Pioneers by Jean Hunt

The Girl Scouts planted "Pride of Hadley" Tulips at the Hockanum Schoolhouse.

FARM TOURS: BARSTOW'S DAIRY, THE HARTSBROOK SCHOOL AND WANCZYK NURSERY

May 3rd featured several more farm tours, a wonderful day out in the Hadley countryside. Touring the farms was impressive and showed the visitors that Hadley farmers are hard working, very knowledgeable and care deeply about the land. Many are descendants of Hadley farmers and have their family's newest generation helping out, carrying on the traditions.

Many people were delighted to visit Barstow's Dairy Store & Bakery at Longview Farm (barstowslongviewfarm.com). This has been a Barstow family farm since 1806, the sixth and seventh generation milk 250 Holsteins. The newest addition to the farm is the Barstow's Dairy Store & Bakery with beautiful views of Mt. Holyoke, and the farm fields and Connecticut River beyond. The store offers sandwiches, soups, salads, light breakfast items and baked goods along with Absolutely Local™ milk & beef. The store also sells local crafts and products, and local artists display their work on the walls each month. Farm Tour participants got a guided tour through the barns and milking parlor, and saw the amazing composting operation using compostable refuse from the store. The tour ended with a free ice cream cone.

Above: The Hartsbrook School henhouse. Below: Cows at the Barstow's Longview Farm.

Top left: Denise Barstow explains the milking parlor. Top right: Hanging plants at Wanczk Nursery. Above left: Touring Barstow's Longview Farm. Above right: Evergreens at Wanczyk Nursery.

Another place people were excited to tour was The Hartsbrook School (hartsbrook.org). It's great to think of the school children caring for the animals and learning about them. Tour visitors got to wander around the farm area, and enjoy the scenic view. As part of their Agricultural Arts Program, the Hartsbrook School offers a series of farm camps for children from the wider community during school vacation weeks. Children work hands-on with a variety of farm animals at the school's farmstead while learning different agricultural crafts.

Lastly, many residents were treated to a visit to Wanczyk Nursery, Inc (wanczyk-nursery.com). A retail and wholesale nursery with over 80 acres in production, Wanczyk's slogan, "We are the growers, come to the source," is familiar to everyone in town. At the open house, visitors were given a guided tour through the nursery, and saw the trees, shrubs, evergreens, perennials, groundcovers and annuals for sale. Visitors left with a better understanding of how the plants are propagated and grown, and how the staff digs the large trees and moves them.

Above left: Entrance to Barstow's Dairy Store. Above right: Marianne Wanczyk explains how the plants are propagated. Below: Hartsbrook School's barnyard.

THE MILLICENT H. KAUFFMAN AWARD FOR DISTINGUISHED SERVICE

The Millicent H. Kauffman Distinguished Service Award is presented by the Amherst Area Chamber of Commerce each year to an individual, group or organization whose work has in some way helped to fulfill the Chamber's mission: "To promote a vital, thriving business climate throughout the Amherst area and to initiate and support the civic, educational, recreational and economic well-being of the Amherst area."

The 2009 award was given jointly to the Hadley 350th Committee and the Amherst 250th Committee at a lovely dinner on May 7. State Representative Ellen Story presented the Committee with a citation from the State Senate and Tony Maroulis, Executive Director of the Amherst Area Chamber of Commerce, presented an inscribed silver plate. The 350th Committee had the two awards framed and presented them to the Hadley Select Board. The awards are currently hanging in town hall.

Below: The 350th Committee accepts the Millicent H. Kauffman Distinguished Service Award from Tony Maroulis, Executive Director, and David Perlmutter, President, of the Amherst Area Chamber of Commerce.

MEMORIAL DAY PARADE

Hadley's annual Memorial Day Parade was much enjoyed. The visits to the town's cemeteries were meaningful, as always, and each stop gathered neighbors to pay tribute to the veterans buried there. The parade was wonderful, and the bands and floats gave a hint of what was to come during the 350th parade.

Top: The 1929 REO Speedwagon was Hadley's first motorized pumper. It was put into service after the flood of 1927 and decommissioned in 1955. Above left: The Hopkins Academy Marching Band, led by director Ed Forman. Above right: Children eagerly collect candies thrown from the floats. Here, Lila West helps her nephew, Tristan.

Clockwise from top: Hadley's Fire Department proudly displays its 2006 Engine 3 Seagraves Marauder II Attack Pumper; Hadley's decorated town hall and library, as well as the Hopkins Academy Marching Band are reflected in Justin Satkowski's sousaphone; veterans from Hadley's American Legion Post 271 lead the parade, followed by Hadley's elected officials. Opposite page: Memorial Day observances in the Hockanum Cemetery.

ANTIQUE TRACTOR SHOW

The farming community of Hadley celebrated the 350th Anniversary by hosting an Antique Tractor Show at The Long Hollow Bison Farm on Sunday, May 24th. The event featured over 120 of the best restored, original and new tractors exhibited for the estimated 4500 hundred people of all ages who came out to support and celebrate the event. The display included tractors from the local fields, barns and farms of Hadley, Hatfield, and Williamsburg to as far away as Maine and Pennsylvania. The Oldest & Rarest Tractor was a 1925 Rumely Oil Pull owned by Bacon's Equipment, Williamsburg, Massachusetts.

The tractors were "judged" by local celebrities and dignitaries, including Hadley Select Board members Gerry Devine, Joyce Chunglo, Brian West and Gloria Difulvio, Springfield Republican publisher Larry McDermott, UMass Basketball Coach Derek Kellogg, veterinarian Dr. Fred Hess, and others.

The event featured over twenty farmers' market vendors, and eleven new equipment dealers. Muddy Brook Farm provided horse drawn wagon rides, Rocky Acre Farms provided a petting zoo and pony rides and Maple Valley 4H provided a raffle table which featured an autographed tractor poster signed by Willy Nelson. There was a trackless train and duck races, face painting and sand art for the kids. Delicious food was available including burgers by Local Burger, ice cream by Flavyors of Cook Farm, hot dogs and cotton candy by the Hadley Park and Recreation, baked potatoes and baked goods by the FFA of Smith Vocational School.

On behalf of the Antique Tractor Committee we would like to extend our most heartfelt appreciation to all those who bought the Antique Tractor banners and to The Springfield Republican, The Valley Advocate, Goulet Trucking Inc., and Whole Foods whose financial and marketing assistance made our event possible.

AWARDS

Best Restoration
1930 International Harvester Farmall,
Tom Perron, Amherst

Best Steel-Wheeled
1932 John Deere GP, Robert MacDonald, Leverett

Best Pre-1960
International Harvester Farmall, Joseph Pelis,
Hatfield

Best Post-1960
1971 Massey Ferguson 1150, Wagner Wood, Amherst

Best in Show
1971 Massey Ferguson 1150, Wagner Wood, Amherst

The favorite entries from Hadley went to:

First Place
Allard's Farms 1952 John Deere A

Second Place
Devine Farms 1934 John Deere A

Third Place
Mapleline Farms 1951 Farmall C

Top: Antique tractors on display. Above: Ed Kelley from Kelley Farm (left) and Martha Boisvert from the North Hadley Sugar Shack (right) participate in the farmers' market at the tractor show.

Working with
years.
WHOLE FOODS

DUCK RACES

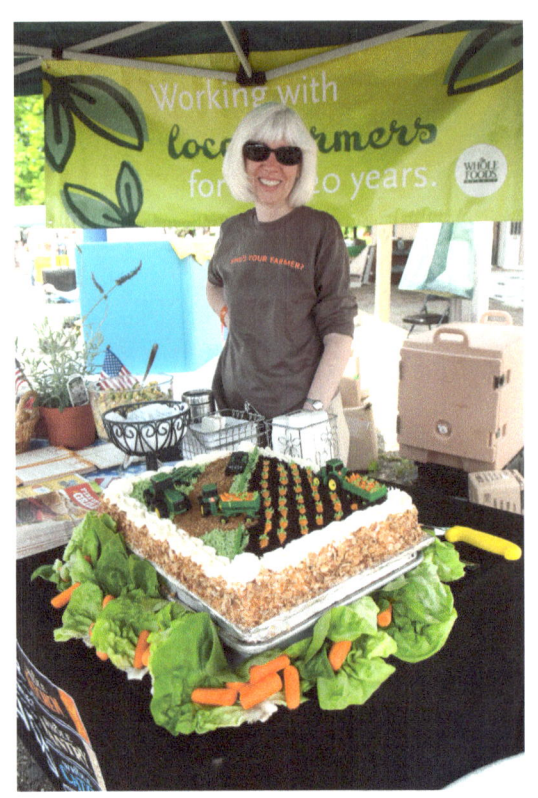

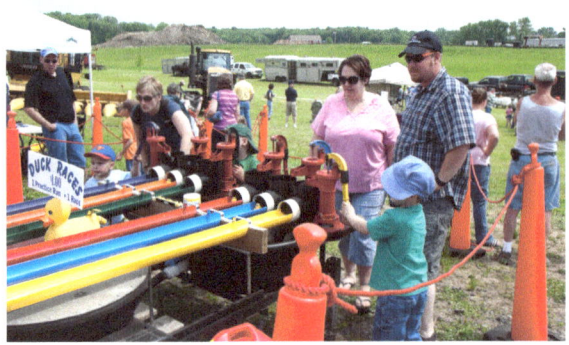

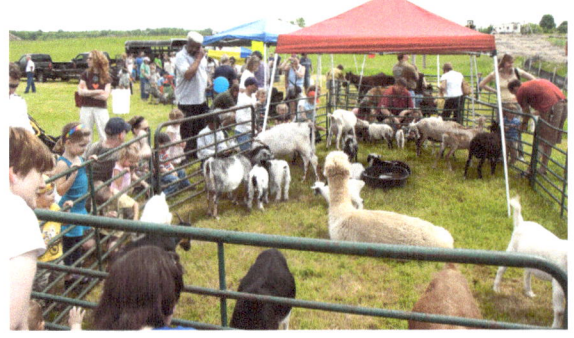

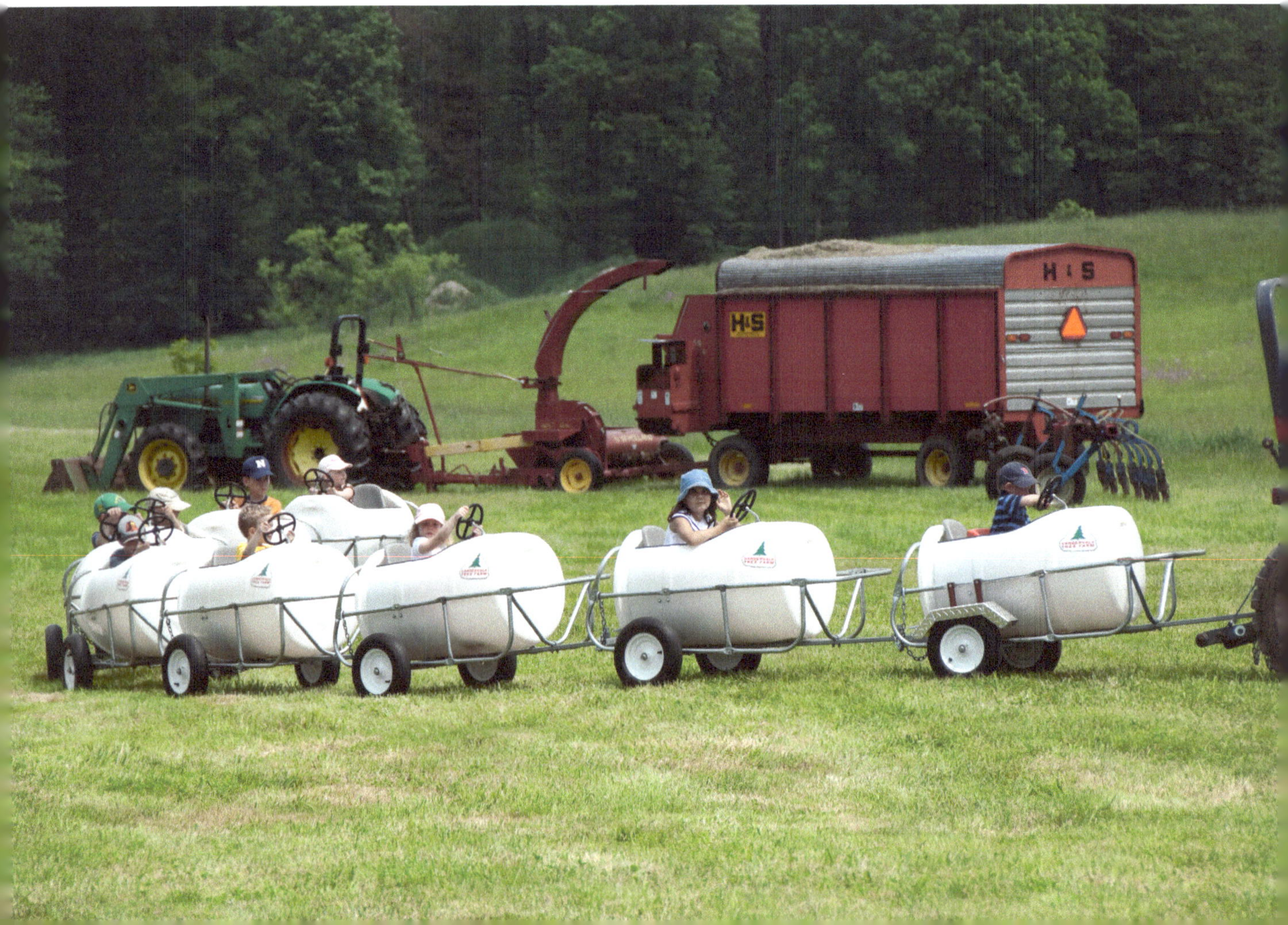
H&S
H&S

Antique Tractor Committee

Bruce Jenks, Allard's Farm Inc., *Committee Chairman*

Tami Kokoski, Mapleline Farm Inc., *Committee Treasurer*

Paul Ciaglo, Long Hollow Bison Farm, *Event Host*

Opposite page, clockwise from top left: Joan Eckert from Whole Foods in Hadley gives out food samples and shares an amazing carrot cake; children enjoy the duck races, petting zoo and trackless train rides at the tractor show. This page: Many types of tractors are on display at the Antique Tractor Show.

SUMMER

Clockwise from top left: Petting zoo at the Firemen's Muster; water lilies on the Artist and Garden Tour; Twin Oaks Farm Tour.

MT. HOLYOKE HIKES

Gini Traub, the Massachusetts Department of Conservation and Recreation's Regional Environmental Education Coordinator-Central West, led three hikes in May and June in the Mt. Holyoke range. The mountain range is an important part of Hadley's past and present, and the hikes were much enjoyed and very informative.

Left: Gini Traub leads a hike on Mt. Holyoke. Top left: Hikers see a lady slipper in bloom. Above: The entrance to Skinner State Park. Opposite page, left: Gini Traub tells about the old auto road. Opposite page, right: The Conglomerate Rock is very interesting to see.

Flowers, Birds, and Trees, Oh My! Enjoying Nature Along the Auto Road at Skinner State Park. This the most magic time of year, at the most magic time of day. Check out what's blooming and budding. Look for and listen to what's singing. The hike will be 3.2 miles round trip, walking up and down the auto road.

Hidden History Along the Auto Road at Skinner State Park. Discover what's left of Mount Holyoke's "other tramway." What event prompted Edward Hitchcock to build the Halfway Trail in 1845? Check out photos of the auto road before the days of pavement and guard rails. We will walk the auto road, well graded and quite steep in places. 3.2 miles round trip plus a .25 mile side trip on a rougher footpath to the remnants of a cabin perched on the side of the mountain.

Fire, Ice and Rocks on the Range: Geology Walk on Trails and Auto Road at Skinner State Park. Volcano and earthquake some 200 million years ago gave the range and valley its basic contours. The ice age smoothed its edges. Wind, weather, freezing and thawing today gives us a landscape that is an unfinished sculpture. Hear the story and see examples as we visit the scalloped and fluted cliff face of Titan's Piazza, the glacial eratics known as Devil's Football and Conglomerate Rock, and enjoy the vista from the mountain's summit. Approximately four miles total, walking on a combination of the paved auto road and somewhat rocky footpaths; both with steep sections.

Top left and right: Astarte Farm. (Photos by Dan Pratt) Above: Rick Thayer takes a break from photographing the Mapleline Farm Tour.

FARM TOURS:
HIBBARD FARM, MAPLELINE FARM AND ASTARTE FARM

The first weekend in June featured tours to three more Hadley farms. Visiting Hibbard Farm was a delight. Sadly, Wally Hibbard passed away shortly after the farm tour. He was a longtime Hadley farmer, and well known for his asparagus and other crops.

Many residents were pleased to get to visit Mapleline Farm (maplelinefarm.com), a fifth-generation dairy farm that specializes in fresh local natural milk with no synthetic growth hormones or additives. As visitors learned, the milk processing and bottling is done right on the farm. Farm visitors were shown through the barns with their herd of Jersey cows, the milking parlor and the bottling plant. Mapleline is one of only a few small milk bottling plants in Massachusetts, and the only one in this area. The Mapleline delivery trucks are a common sight in town, as the farm offers home delivery of milk, cheese, yogurt, ice cream, frozen beef and other products to Hadley and eight surrounding towns. Their products are also available in many local stores. Visitors ended the tour with a sample of one of the flavored milks Mapleline offers—a real treat.

Another interesting open house was at Astarte Farm (astartefarm.com). A highly diversified certified organic market garden located at one of the original farms in Hadley, they specialize in heirloom tomatoes (both plants and fruit), unusual lettuce varieties, sweet corn, and fresh cut flowers with an arugula to zucchini mix to fill in the gaps. They pick all of their varieties for superior taste, try to source organic seed whenever possible, and even grow a few outstanding hybrids.

Top: Mapleline Farm truck. Below left: John Kokoski explains Mapleline's milking parlor. Below right: Wally Hibbard selling asparagus. (Photo by Marge Barrett-Mills)

HADLEY 350TH PHOTO EXHIBIT CONTEST AND HERITAGE DISPLAY

The Hadley 350th Photo Exhibit Committee invited area residents to contribute to a display of photographs (both historical and new work) celebrating the beauty, diversity and richness of Hadley's heritage. The array of photographs in the exhibit was amazing, from small snapshots of children and animals to stunning landscapes, rainbows, barns and evocative black-and-white prints. The site of the exhibit was the Summit House on the top of Mt. Holyoke and it was an outstanding location. The photographs filled the large airy rooms and brightened up the spacious interior of the historic building. A crowded event on June 7th officially opened the exhibit to the public, but the photos remained on display from Memorial Day to Labor Day, which allowed everyone the entire summer to visit the exhibit and enjoy the artwork.

There were more than 300 photographs in the exhibit, reflecting an image of the community, its land or its people. Of these, approximately 100 were historical prints depicting Hadley buildings and landscapes, events like floods, or agriculture in olden days. Approximately sixty individuals overall submitted work; fourteen prizes were awarded to the winners in different categories. Visitors flocked to the Summit House throughout the summer months in 2009 to view the exhibit and many returned more than once to take it all in. We were fortunate that so many talented photographers generously shared their creative work with us and allowed us to visually enjoy the many facets of our community's beauty.

> ### Contest Winners
>
> *First Place*
> HERITAGE: William Dwyer, "Flood" Collage
> PROFESSIONAL: Eric Poggenpohl, "Seven Sisters Mountain Range, Hadley, Massachusetts"
> AMATEUR: Donald David, "Proud Heritage"
> JUNIOR: Emily Bernotas, "Fisherman"
>
> *Second Place*
> AMATEUR: Elaine Mishkind, "Pastoral Tranquility"
> AMATEUR: Sandra Pipczynski, "Asparagus Bunches"
> JUNIOR: Catherine Futter, "Old Barn"
>
> *Third Place*
> AMATEUR: Jerry Gabriel, "North Hadley Pond 2002"
> AMATEUR: Alfred Hutt, "Got Milk"
> AMATEUR: Christine Wu, "Morning Mist Lake Warner (B)
>
> *Fourth Place*
> AMATEUR: Mary Barnett, "Laundry Day"
> AMATEUR: Marge Barrett-Mills, "Cook Farm #2"
> AMATEUR: Connie Degnan, "Soft Landing"
> AMATEUR: Andy Morris-Friedman, "Connecticut River Flood"

Opposite page: Opening reception of the Photo Exhibit Contest and Heritage Displays at the Summit House. (Top left photo by Patsy Lewis)

HADLEY'S 350TH ANNIVERSARY
PHOTO EXHIBIT CONTEST & HERITAGE DISPLAYS
SPONSORED BY
PeoplesBank
Great relationships start here.
OPENING RECEPTION: SUNDAY, JUNE 7TH 1:00 -- 4:00 PM

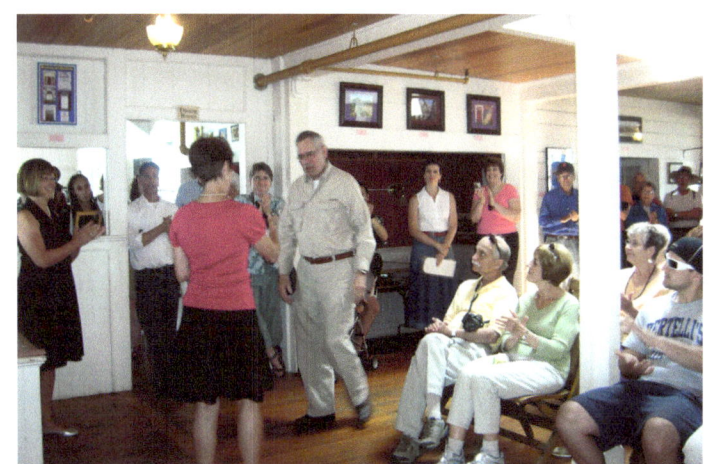

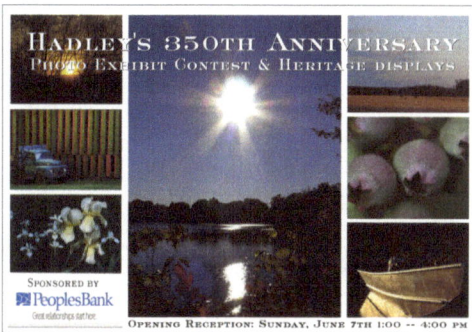

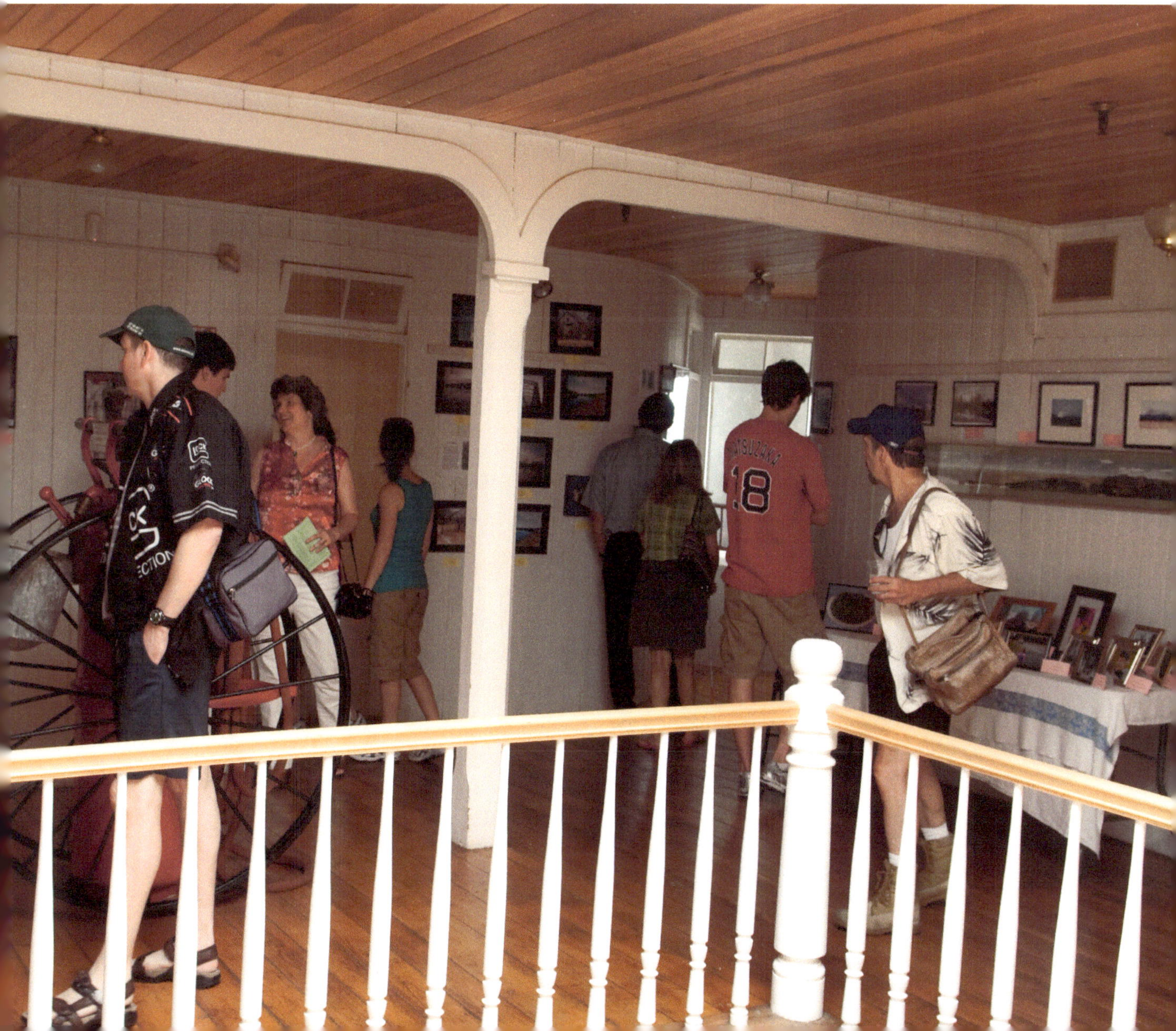

18

RIDING TOUR OF WEST STREET COMMON

An early 1900s photo of the McQueston home on West Street. (Photo courtesy of Ted McQueston)

The Hadley Historical Society offered a riding tour of the West Street Common with a brief history of the architectural design and ownership of older homes. Gladys Kozera, a long time resident of West Street, was the tour guide. Gladys had many family members residing on West Street and had many tales to tell. The tour, in a van provided by the Council on Aging, stopped in front of the oldest home on West Street, presently owned by Ted McQueston and dating back to 1713. The tour also stopped by the birthplace of General Joseph Hooker.

The event consisted of two tours to accommodate the people wanting to view the homes. Some of the guests once lived on West Street and enjoyed reminiscing about their childhood days. At the end of the tour, the visitors had an opportunity to ask questions regarding the older homes. Many of the questions were informative and provided detailed historical facts.

The program was very successful and a recorded tape was made of the tour.

HISTORICAL SOCIETY OPEN HOUSE

On June 13th, the Hadley Historical Society opened the Museum room on the second floor of the Goodwin Memorial Libary to the public. The museum is filled with many items from Hadley's history including photos, letters, clothing, household items, memorabilia, documents, genealogical information, war memorabilia, furniture and more. There are so many interesting items to see, and the items tell a lot about Hadley's past. Along with the Museum room, the Hadley Historical Society holds regular meetings and presents programs of historical interest for the public. During the 350th celebration, several donations were made to the Society's collection, which have added to the preservation of Hadley's history.

The Museum Room on the second floor of the Goodwin Memorial Library.

HOPKINS ACADEMY ALL CLASS REUNION

More than four hundred alumni and guests attended the Hopkins Acadmey all-class reunion, held at the Young Men's Club the evening before the big 350th parade. President Bernadette Pipczynski Wyman welcomed everyone to the celebration of the 345th anniversary of Hopkins Academy. She introduced Robert Barrett from the class of 1958, who gave the invocation. Diana Bonneville, the Academy's current Principal, reminded the group that Hopkins is the seventh oldest school in New England and one of the ten oldest schools in the United States.

The reunion was a great success and a wonderful start to the celebration weekend. The next reunion will be held in 2014 and will commemorate the 350th anniversary of the founding of Hopkins Academy (www.hopkinsalumni.org).

> **THE ALUMNI ASSOCIATION OF HOPKINS ACADEMY**
>
> BERNADETTE PIPCZYNSKI WYMAN, *President*
> CONSTANCE PAULSON MIECZKOWSKI, *Vice President*
> JANINE THOMAS GILES, *Treasurer*
> KATHLEEN TUDRYN, *Secretary*

Hopkins Academy all class reunion at the Young Men's Club. (Photo courtesy of the Hopkins Academy Alumni Association)

Left: Class of 1960, left to right standing: Al Kulas, Richard Yarrows, Pat Kielbowicz Zumbruski, Bernie Pipczynski Wyman, Marion Kostek Waskiewicz. Left to right front row: Louise Moczulewski Olbris, Leona Waskiewicz Chmura, Diane Kozera Baj and Lorraine Michalowski Zieminski. Below: Hopkins graduates young and old alike enjoyed the festivities and reconnecting with school friends. (Photos courtesy of the Hopkins Academy Alumni Association)

SUMMER 53

350TH PARADE

Hadley's 350th parade was held on Sunday, June 14, 2009, and was enjoyed by an appreciative and enthusiastic crowd. As the town awoke to a light drizzle, people nervously watched the skies, but just as the parade commenced, the clouds cleared and we all enjoyed a beautiful day. The two-hour parade began on Russell Street (Route 9) at the Mill Valley Road intersection and traveled west down Russell Street to the West Street Common (1.8 miles). The parade consisted of approximately 1200 participants in twenty bands, more than thirty floats, over 200 Shriners, antique bicycles, trucks, tractors, farm equipment, automobiles, and much, much more. Terry Warner and Scott Harris announced over 100 parade units from the viewing stand set up next to Town Hall. John Koloski was the Grand Marshall, and rode the parade route on top of the Farm Museum's stage coach.

Thanks go out to the Parade Committee for their thought, care, and preparation, and for working so diligently for the past three years to put together this fantastic memorable event. They couldn't have done it without the terrific help from all the volunteers on the day of the parade which included their family members, Hadley friends, members of the Hadley Fire Department (who manned the emergency stations), the Hadley Police Department, who, along with police from surrounding towns, kept traffic running smoothly, the Hampshire County Sheriffs who parked cars, and the Hadley Highway Department for all of the rapid cleanup work. And special thanks to Easthampton Savings Bank, the main parade sponsor and to all the parade sponsors.

Parade Committee: left to right standing, Chris Hopkins, John Kieras, Chip Parsons (co-chair), Norm Barstow (co-chair), John Koloski, David Fill, Michael Spanknebel, Alan Jacque; left to right seated, Carla Grabiec, Sharon Parsons, Janet Barstow, Joyce Fill, Dennis Hukowicz, Jessica Spanknebel.

The post parade party at the Young Men's Club was greatly enjoyed. (Photos by Gerry Delisle)

Tens of thousands of people celebrated with Hadley on this memorable day.

The Young Men's Club hosted a free party at their pavilion following the parade. Many of the parade participants and viewers enjoyed their hospitality. The YMC added to the community spirit of the day.

A Parade Photo Book and a DVD were produced to help memorialize this wonderful day. The photo book contains over 300 photos on 106 pages, and includes a description of each unit in the parade. The DVD includes the entire parade with the announcers' commentary.

Top: The Hopkins Academy Marching Band. (Photo by Jerry Gabriel) Above: The First Congregational Church of Hadley's float.

Top: The Hadley Public Schools' float. Above: The Hadley Council on Aging's float. (Photos by Jerry Gabriel)

Top: The Alumni Association of Hopkins Academy's float. (Photo by Jerry Gabriel) Above: The Boisvert Farm's float.

Top: The Hadley Fire Department. Above: The Hartsbrook Farm's float. (Photo by Josh Thayer)

List of Parade Units

Hadley American Legion Post #271, Hadley Police Department, Hadley Fire Department and Color Guard, Parade Marshal John Koloski in 1848 Abbot Stage Coach, Hopkins Academy Marching Band, Alumni Association of Hopkins Academy, Mrs. Victoria Kozera Drabek (oldest citizen in town), Hadley Council on Aging, Muddy Brook Farm, Hampshire County Farm Bureau, Dicey Riley Irish Band and the Kelley Farm, Hockanum Villagers Association, Current or Former Hadley Selectmen, Western Mass. Model T. Club, Hadley Fire Department, Hopkins Academy Graduating Class of 1959, Polish American Citizens Club, Hadley Historical Society, William Smith, Hadley Historical Commission, John Kieras, Wethersfield, CT Police Department, Wethersfield Volunteer Fire Department, Windsor Fife & Drum Corps., Hadley Public Schools, Misty Meadow Farm, Department of Conservation and Recreation (DCR) and Department of Civilian Conservation Corps. (CCC), Leverett Fire Department and Leverett Police Cruiser, Mapleline Farm, Excelsior Drum and Bugle Corps., Frank R. Blajda, Elected Officials, Hampshire County Sheriff's Department, Westhampton Fire Department, University of Massachusetts Police Department, Ancient Mariners (Connecticut Fife and Drum Corps), Hadley Lions Club, Whole Foods Market, Amherst Town Officials, Amherst Police Department, Amherst Fire Department, Marquis of Granby Junior Fyfe and Drum Corps, Amherst College Campus Police, Norm's Auto Body, First Congregational Church of Hadley, Hadley Girl Scouts, Wanczyk Nursery, Wesley United Methodist Church, Greenfield Fire Department, Massachusetts State Police, North Hadley Sugar Shack, Polish Heritage Company, Florence Community Band, Hampshire, Franklin and Hampden Agricultural Society (Three County Fair), Easthampton Fire Department, Hampshire Lodge of Masons, Hampshire Council of Government, Royer Family, Holyoke High School Band, Belchertown Twirlers, Doubleday Farms, Northampton St. Patrick's Association and Northampton Fire Department, 10th MA Volunteer Militia, Boisvert Farm, Gary Berg, Sunderland Fire Department, Hartsbrook Farm and Cook Farm, Drozdal Family, Valley Vodka, Marksman Alumni Drum and Bugle Corps, Freedom Fighter Foundation, Tally-Ho 4-H Horse Club, Atkins Farms Country Market, Warehouse Point Ancient Fife and Drum Corps, Boy Scout Troop #504, Eastern States Exposition, Sunderland Selectmen, Waltham American Legion Band, State Forest Fire Control—District 10 and Goshen Fire Department, Czelusniak Funeral Home of Northampton, Amherst 250th Anniversary Celebration Committee, Banish Misfortune Irish Band, David Johnson Family, Huntington Fire Department, South Hadley Selectmen, Hatfield Historical Society, Quaboag Highlanders Pipe Band, Korean War Veterans Association, American Truck Historical Society, North County Line Dancers, Whately Fire Department, Hatfield Hellion Car/Truck, Granby Police Department, South Hadley St. Patrick's Parade Committee, Glenn Loud, Hatfield Selectmen and Hatfield Fire Department, Allard's Farm, Williamsburg Fire Department, Melha Shrine Band, Allard Farm's Combine.

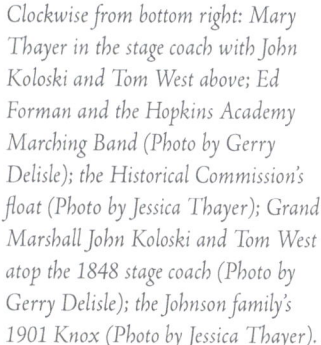

Clockwise from bottom right: Mary Thayer in the stage coach with John Koloski and Tom West above; Ed Forman and the Hopkins Academy Marching Band (Photo by Gerry Delisle); the Historical Commission's float (Photo by Jessica Thayer); Grand Marshall John Koloski and Tom West atop the 1848 stage coach (Photo by Gerry Delisle); the Johnson family's 1901 Knox (Photo by Jessica Thayer).

SUMMER 61

Clockwise from top left: The first three photos are of the party at the Young Men's Club (photos by Gerry Delisle); the Souvenir Shoppe is open parade day in the Town Hall (photo by Gerry Delisle); John Vassallo, manager of the Hadley Easthampton Savings Bank branch and the treasurer of the 350th Committee, sells Souvenir Guides during the parade (photo by Tom Brown). Opposite page: Governor Deval Patrick's Proclamation.

Commonwealth of Massachusetts

A Proclamation

His Excellency Governor Deval L. Patrick

Whereas Reverend John Russell and his dissenting Puritan congregation of Connecticut settled Hadley in 1659 as an agricultural community on the east bank of the Connecticut River; and

Whereas Hadley was incorporated in 1661; and

Whereas According to legend, during King Philip's War, the town was saved from destruction when, William Goffe, one of the English judges who sentenced King Charles I to death and later fled to New England when the English monarchy was restored in 1660, warned of the danger, and led the town in fending off the assault and disappeared shortly afterward. Since then, he has been referred to as the "Angel of Hadley" for his efforts in saving the town; and

Whereas Since its establishment, Hadley has been a leader in agriculture. After the Revolution, broomcorn became its dominant crop, and the town became the nation's broom manufacturing capital. By the 1840s, tobacco replaced broomcorn and by 1920, Hadley had become the asparagus capital of the world; and

Whereas Throughout our history, the men and women of Hadley have answered the call of duty and served in our armed forces; and

Whereas We congratulate the Town of Hadley and its citizens upon the 350th anniversary of its incorporation and extend greetings as they gather to celebrate this important milestone in their history,

Now, Therefore, I, Deval L. Patrick, Governor of the Commonwealth of Massachusetts, do hereby proclaim June 14th, 2009, to be

HADLEY DAY

And urge all the citizens of the Commonwealth to take cognizance of this event and participate fittingly in its observance.

Given at the Executive Chamber in Boston, this first day of June, in the year two thousand and nine, and of the Independence of the United States of America, the two hundred and thirty-second.

By His Excellency

DEVAL L. PATRICK
GOVERNOR OF THE COMMONWEALTH

WILLIAM FRANCIS GALVIN
SECRETARY OF THE COMMONWEALTH

God Save the Commonwealth of Massachusetts

HOUSE DECORATING CONTEST

Just as in celebrations past, Hadley's town buildings were decorated with banners and bunting. To help create a festive mood across the comunity, Hadley Park and Recreation sponsored a house-decorating contest between May 24th and July 4th. The Hadley 350th Committee was grateful to the select board members from our daughter towns who agreed to serve as judges: Jim Hines of South Hadley, Stephanie O'Keefe of Amherst, and Jeff Boyle of Hatfield. There were many wonderfully decorated homes and businesses throughout the town. Mary and Rick Thayer of Hockanum Road took home the award for "Most Patriotic," while "Best Historical Theme" went to Ed Mokrzecky of River Drive, with Carmelina's Restaurant supplying the prizes.

Russell School decorated for the 350th.

Left: The Senior Center (Hooker School) decorated for the 350th.
Top: Thayer home won "Most Patriotic." Above: Mokrzecky home won "Best Historical Theme."

JULY 4TH FIREWORKS

The Hadley 350th Committee and the Amherst 250th Committee jointly sponsored fireworks at the annual 4th of July celebration at the University of Massachusetts Amherst stadium to create the biggest display ever. At 6:30 PM, there was a joint birthday celebration, with a barbershop quartet, clowns, a pie-eating contest and more. Prizes were given away to those who could answer Hadley trivia questions. The fireworks dazzled the large crowd and were watched from many backyards in Hadley, too.

There were extra special fireworks on July 4th at UMass in honor of Hadley's 350th and Amherst's 250th.

CELEBRATING HADLEY'S APR LEADERSHIP

On July 7, officials of the Massachusetts Department of Agricultural Resources (DAR) joined local farmers, and land trusts, landowners and municipal officials to celebrate the town of Hadley's achievement in protecting more farmland than any other community in the state.

"It's an honor to be here, celebrating the immense success and commitment of the town of Hadley toward protecting agricultural land in our Commonwealth," said DAR Commissioner Scott Soares. "I encourage communities throughout Massachusetts to strive toward maximizing farm land protection and look forward to working with our municipal partners toward preservation of our precious working landscapes."

Through DAR's Agricultural Preservation Restriction (APR) Program, Hadley has protected more than 2,400 acres of farmland, including 149 acres at seven farms this summer. "Our goal is to protect at least 4,000 acres of farmland," said Alexandra Dawson, Chair of the Hadley Conservation Commission. "Hadley got its start as a farming community and 350 years later it is still a farming community. We hope it will stay that way for centuries to come."

The APR Program pays agricultural landowners the difference between their land's fair market value and its agricultural value in exchange for a permanent deed restriction precluding any future use of the property that would harm its agricultural viability. The voluntary program provides an economic incentive for farmers to keep their property as farmland, rather than sell it for development.

When the program began in 1979, it was the first of its kind in the nation; many other states have used it as a model since then. The primary purpose of the APR program is to preserve and protect agricultural land, including designated farmland soils—a finite natural resource—from being built upon for non-agricultural purposes or used for any activity detrimental to agriculture. As of 2008, the APR program had permanently preserved more than 725 farms and 61,855 acres of agricultural lands statewide.

Public funding to acquire the Hadley APRs was provided by DAR, the U.S. Department of Agriculture Natural Resources Conservation Service, Hadley's Community Preservation Act and other town funds, as well as private grants from land trusts: The Kestrel Trust, Valley Land Fund, Open Space Institute, and The Trustees of Reservations.

During the town's celebration commemorating its 350th anniversary, protected farms displayed "Forever Farmland" signs. The Kestrel Trust, farmers and town officials teamed up to display the signs, which guide viewers to the website, foreverfarmland.org.

Top: Forever Farmland signs can be seen all over town on preserved farmland.

HADLEY ART EXHIBIT IN THE CORN BARN OF THE PORTER-PHELPS-HUNTINGTON HOUSE

Hadley's 350th celebration was a great year for the visual arts in town. In addition to the photography exhibit, other events showcased painters. There had not been a group of Hadley artists exhibiting here together since the 1970s (HPIA, Hadley People Interested in the Arts), but three events brought together the work of artists who were Hadley natives, artists who now reside in Hadley, or artists who had lived here for a number of years and have moved to local towns: an exhibit in the Corn Barn of the Porter-Phelps-Huntington House in July, the Garden Tour and Artist Festival on July 18, and the "350 x 24" art exhibit at the U.S. Fish & Wildlife Building during November and December (described under fall events, below).

"New Work by Hadley Artists" occurred throughout July in the Corn Barn of the Porter-Phelps-Huntington Museum. This was the first time that a group of Hadley artists displayed at the museum. The event was organized by John Romanski, originally from Brooklyn, New York, who has lived in Hadley for a few years. John wanted to bring art into the local community and place it in a familiar setting. The Corn Barn seemed to be a perfect alternative gallery space. Local artists Steve and Elizabeth Wilda designed the advertising material. Nancy Fernald, Rita Edelman and John Romanski hung the artwork submitted by Rita Edelman, Jacob Elmets, Nancy Fernald, Nadine Gallo, Barbara Johnson, Karen Leveille, Diane Nevinsmith, Sandra Pipczynski, John Romanski, Elizabeth Wilda, Fred Wilda and Steve Wilda. The opening reception was held on July 5th, the same day as "Hadley Day" at Porter-Phelps-Huntington Museum, and was well attended. Refreshments were coordinated by Jane Nevinsmith.

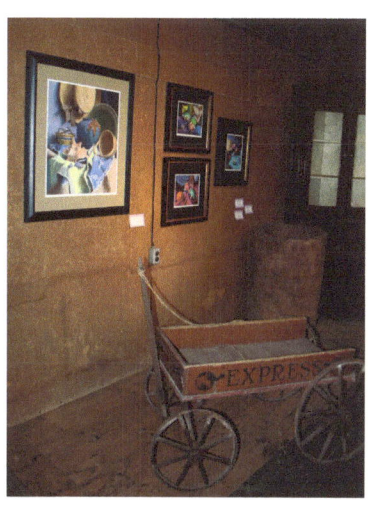

Art Exhibit in the Corn Barn. (Photos by Steve Wilda)

GARDEN AND ARTIST TOUR, ARTIST FESTIVAL

Another successful event to celebrate the arts was the Garden and Artist tour. Many enjoyed the scenic back roads of Hadley on this self-guided tour of eleven beautiful gardens, three artist studios, an art festival at a local historic church, and a food and rest stop at Barstow's Longview Farm on Route 47. Whether capturing Hadley's beauty on canvas, by camera, in the creative designs of a quilt or jewelry, or by working in Hadley's famous soil creating flower and vegetable gardens, over 300 people from Hadley and area towns experienced creativity at its finest. They visited and talked with the artists and gardeners at each location, stopping along the way to enjoy the bucolic views or have a picnic. Several people from nearby towns were heard to say "I never knew how beautiful Hadley was," as they saw one incredible vista after another.

Artists were stationed in a number of locations for the public to enjoy their work. Rita Edelman and Nancy Fernald both had open studios at their homes. Lewis Bryden was also on the tour with his open studio/boat, providing rides on the Connecticut River. Organizer Debbie Windoloski's garden tour stop hosted Robin Keller and John Romanski's art on display. Nine additional Hadley artists exhibited their art in The First Congregational Church on Middle Street, among them art event organizers Steve and Elizabeth Wilda. The Artist and Garden Tour was a tremendous success with the public, sure to inspire future tours.

Garden Tour
Betsy Alden
Irene Bercume
Sally and Michael Farnham
Jim and Gerry Harvey
Gene Hoynoski
Susan Russell
Mary Thayer
Rebecca and Mark Uchneat
Frank and Joanne Wilda
Debbie Windoloski
Jacqui Zuzgo

Top: A water lily in the Thayer garden. Left: Nadine Gallo talks to Steve Wilda beside his artwork. (Photo by Sandra Pipczynski)

Left: Flowers delight visitors in the Harvey garden. Right: Elizabeth Wilda displays her photographs. (Photo by Sandra Pipczynski) Below: A beautiful border in the Russell garden.

Clockwise from top left: A water lily from the Thayer garden; visitors enjoy the Harvey gardens; a beautiful scene from the Russell garden; the fish pond at the Windoloski garden.

On the garden tour, visitors enjoyed the pond at the Thayer home (above) and the gardens at the Russell home (below).

Open Studio Artists
Lewis Bryden
Rita Edelman
Nancy Fernald

Garden Artists
Robin Keller
John Romanski

First Church Artists
Nadine Gallo
John Gnatek
Patricia Czepiel Hayes
Barbara Johnson
Sandra Pipczynski
Helen Rodak
Elizabeth Wilda
Fred Wilda
Steve Wilda

FARM TOURS: GREAT MEADOW FRUITS, HARTSBROOK FARM, PLAINVILLE FARM AND TWIN OAKS FARM

The last week in July featured several more wonderful farm tours. The visit to Great Meadow Fruits (czajkowskifarm.com), Joe Czajkowski's farm, showcased the tasty blueberries, raspberries, peaches and blackberries available "you pick" and already picked, at his farm land in the Great Meadow. Tour visitors could walk up and down the rows of fruit shrubs and trees, enjoying the beauty of the Great Meadow, and the colors of the ripe fruits.

At Hartsbrook Farm, founded in the early 1800s by Thomas West, the sixth and seventh generation now work the land. Visitors learned about their 200 Registered Holsteins, dairy and breeding stock. Art West greeted visitors and showed them the main barn, proudly talking about his family farm. His young grandchildren were nearby, watching the new born calves.

Plainville Farm grows 120 acres of vegetables and tobacco. Guests at the farm tour learned how the Walter Czajkowski family grows the lettuce, asparagus, tomatoes, cabbage, pickling cucumbers, organic green and yellow beans, and many varieties of winter squash and pumpkins harvested all summer and fall. Plainville Farm also peels and packs butternut squash. Their broad leaf tobacco is used for cigar wrappers and sold worldwide. The cooler was stacked high with crates of beans and cabbages. It was very interesting to see the machinery used to sort the beans. The samples of pickles to try were a treat.

At Twin Oaks Farm, a third generation mixed vegetable farm located at the end of Stockbridge Street, the major crops are butternut squash, summer squash, zucchini, cabbage, peppers and Indian corn. They also grow leeks, beets, eggplant and mini pumpkins. The Matuszkos treated visitors to a wagon ride through their fields and neighboring farmers' fields, explaining what was being grown and answering lots of questions. One of their barns had a nice display set up with the history of the farm, information on their farming products, farming memorabilia and baskets of farm produce worthy of an entry in a country fair. There were delicious goodies, too.

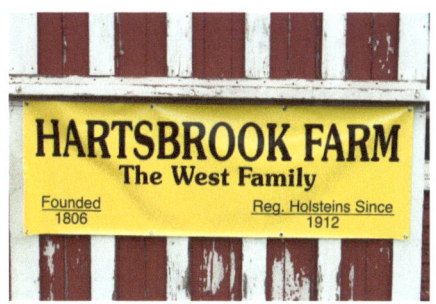

Opposite page: View from the Matuszko's Twin Oaks Farm tour. Top left: A cow watches the visitors coming to the West Farm. Top right: Hartsbrook Farm on Bay Road. Ripe peaches are plentiful at the Great Meadow Fruits farm. Above: Wally Czajkowski shows the virus attacking the tobacco crop. No tobacco was harvested successfully in Hadley this year; all was lost.

EDDIE FORMAN ORCHESTRA POLKA PARTY

Held on Saturday August 8 in the Young Men's Club Pavilion, this was a very special celebration for the town of Hadley. The Eddie Forman Orchestra is an outstanding group of musicians who are famous in the local area and beyond for their repertoire of polka music and professional performances. They have a loyal and devoted following who filled the Young Men's Club that night to enjoy the music and dancing and the special atmosphere that EFO creates.

Eddie Forman is a unique part of the Hadley community. Born and raised in Hadley, he started his first band while a student at Hopkins Academy and he has been performing music ever since. As the present Hopkins Academy music teacher and director of the marching and jazz bands, he has won numerous awards, most notably in Florida on one of his frequent trips with the band to march in the Disney World parades. His own prowess as a musician, composer and orchestra leader was recognized in 2006 when he was inducted into the International Polka Music Hall of Fame.

It was an honor to have such a fine and dedicated musician celebrating all that is best in the community of Hadley. August 8th was a night to celebrate our town's Polish heritage with all generations enjoying polka dancing and the lively music. It was also a night to celebrate the vibrant community spirit that is being passed along to future generations.

The Eddie Forman Orchestra left to right: Frank Kolodzieski, Bob Frydryk, Lenny Kokoski, Charlie Pajak, Eddie Forman, and John Cieplik on drums in the back.

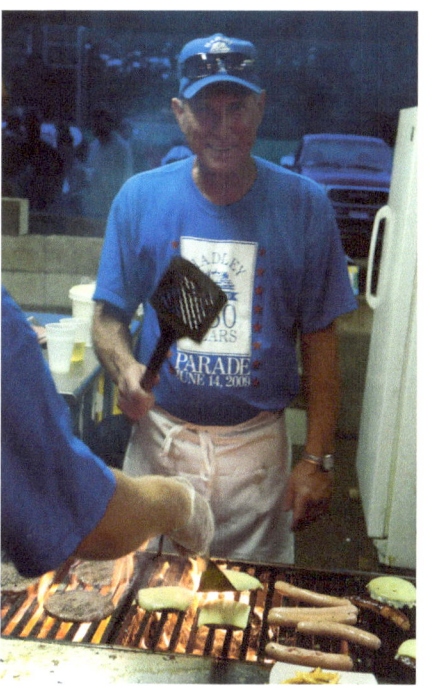

The Eddie Forman Orchestra delighted the crowd at the Young Men's Club. Top right: Pete Laurenza grilling up a feast.

GIRL SCOUT OUTDOOR MOVIE NIGHT

The outdoor family movie night at the Hadley Elementary School was organized by the Hadley Girl Scouts. "Hotel for Dogs" (rated PG) was shown on a huge inflatable outdoor movie screen on the playing fields. Popcorn, snacks and glow sticks were available for sale by the Girl Scouts. Many of the 200 who came enjoyed face painting, children's activities and playing on the playground before the movie started. It was a fun, family event.

Above and left: Face painting by Hadley girl scouts is popular. Far left: Watching the huge movie screen inflating was part of the fun.

HADLEY SAMPLER:
AN ANNIVERSARY CELEBRATION, 1659–2009

In August, working in collaboration with members of Hadley's 350th and Publications Committees, Historic Deerfield recognized Hadley's anniversary and the town's important role in the Connecticut River Valley by mounting an exhibition featuring noteworthy objects associated with Hadley from their collection. The artifacts gathered together in the lobby of the Flynt Center of Early New England Life captured moments in the history of the town—both in the 18th and 19th centuries, when residents made and acquired these objects, and also in the 20th and 21st centuries, when descendants lovingly placed them in museums to ensure their preservation.

The exhibition, curated by Smith College intern Alison Tebaldi, invited visitors to contemplate the values, preferences, and priorities that shaped the production and purchase of these articles in their day, as well as the sentiments that encouraged their latter-day owners to cherish and preserve them. It featured, among other things, a tall case clock made by Hadley craftsman Elijah Yeomans, a 1770s banister chair made by Samuel Gaylord, Jr., an embroidered crewel work ladies pocket by Matilda Cook, a sampler made by Abigail Cook when she attended Miss Pollina Sellon's School, c. 1825, an 1820s silk dress from Hadley, and a chair made by Samuel Gaylord, some ceramics owned by Charles Phelps Jr. and his wife Elizabeth Porter Phelps of Forty Acres, and a brown silk taffeta gown worn by Lizzie Scott Nash in 1881 and recently donated to Historic Deerfield by Alice Nash. The exhibit ran through the end of January. A catalog of the exhibit with color images of each item is available in the Historic Deerfield museum store.

1825 sampler by ten-year-old Hadleyh resident Abigail F. Cook while at Miss Pollina Sellon's school. (Photo by Penny Leveritt; photo courtesy of Historic Deerfield)

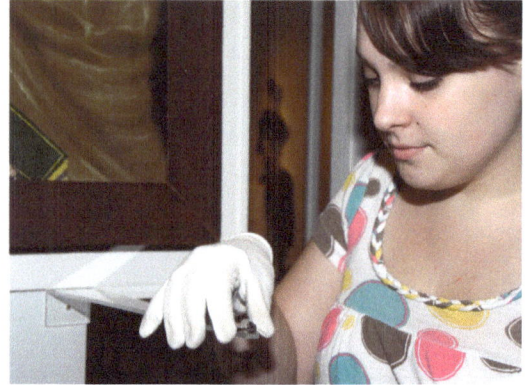

Clockwise from left: 1881 Nash family dress; one of the famed "Hadley" carved chests (1715–1720); Alison Tebaldi at work; 1836 portrait of Mary Jones by Erastus Salisbury Field. (Photos courtesy of Historic Deerfield. Photo of chest by Amanda Merullo, others by Penny Leveritt.)

BLOCK PARTY

On September 12th, a huge tent was set up in the parking lot of the American Legion, and people had a great time dancing to the music of "Mark VI," an old-time polka band, followed by the "Skidmarks," an oldies band. The food was delicious and the music was fabulous.

Top left: Sam and Sue Russell enjoy the dance. Top middle: Mark Uchneat and his son Nicholas dance to the music. Top right: Kris Beaudry of Sophia's Polish-American Café serves up delicious food. Above: The Skidmarks delight the crowd.

FIREMEN'S MUSTER

The Firemen's Muster took place on the Town Common, to the delight of the crowd. The event started with a parade of fire trucks from the Hadley Fire Department, and then the muster got underway. The Hadley Fire Department hosted the event, setting up each of the classes. The classes were Midnight Alarm, Moving Motor Hose, Pumping, Hilltop Pumping, and Oil Fire. The competitors were volunteer firemen from Hinsdale, Hatfield, Bissellville, and Whately. The event was organized by Ken Rodak, and coordinated by Whately Fire Chief John Hannum. Neither the competitors nor the crowd were deterred by the drizzle or mud. It was amazing to see the antique trucks in action, and the crowd got an appreciation for how much skill and strength it took to compete. Young and old enjoyed the activities provided by the Hadley Park and Recreation Department and the Boisverts Farm. There were duck races, tractor rides and animals on display. The event was sponsored by the Hadley 350th Committee, the Five College Credit Union and two golf tournaments held earlier that Ken Rodak had organized. Firemen's Musters used to be a common event in Hadley, and many were glad to see the event brought back for the 350th celebration.

Opposite page: The Hindsdale team competes in the Oil Fire Drill. Top and middle: Teams compete on the common in the various drills. Above left: The crowd cheers the teams. Above right: Children enjoy the duck races and other activities set up on the Common.

FARM TOURS: COOK FARM'S 100th, NORTH HADLEY SUGAR SHACK AND THE FOOD BANK FARM

There were three final farm tours in September. Cook Farm & Flavyors of Cook Farm (cookfarm.com) had a very special 100th anniversary celebration at their farm. Founded in 1909, today fourth and fifth generation Cooks work the farm and the ice cream shop. They raise their own dairy feed and also straw and hay for sale. They sell dairy products including ice cream and raw milk, and in the spring, composted manure. The ice cream shop is a favorite for sandwiches and soups, too. And the monthly flavor of ice cream is always a treat—even the asparagus ice cream! To celebrate the farm's centennial year, Gordon Cook welcomed the large audience and told about the history of the family farm. U.S. Representative Richard Neal and State Representative John Scibak congratulated the Cooks, as did Selectman Gerry Devine and 350th Co-Chair Mary Thayer. Representatives from farm agencies spoke of the farm's contributions and successes. There were many family activities which were well enjoyed. The food—especially the ice cream—was tops.

The North Hadley Sugar Shack at Boisvert Farm (northhadleysugarshack.com) again opened its doors and farm for a fall tour. Their farm store and yard were brimming with pumpkins, squash, mums, asters, garlic, onions, corn stalks and potatoes. It was fun to see the crates full of produce in the storage barns and the building where the maple syrup is bottled and the maple candy is made. Fall molds were being used to create the delicious candies. Children were delighted with the petting zoo. The tour included a hay wagon ride to their corn maze on Mt. Warner Road.

The Food Bank Farm opened their farm store and farm during the week to the public. Visitors got to see the farm store and could wander through the acres of flowers and crops. They got a sense of the close connection the members felt towards the farm and the food grown there. The Food Bank Farm grows an assortment of organic vegetable for its 700 member CSA. It produces a variety of organic salad dressings, pestos and baked goods and sells many local products in its farm store. The farm donates around 200,000 pounds of organic produce to The Food Bank each year. Note, The Food Bank of Western Massachusetts closed The Food Bank Farm at the end of 2009; the CSA farm will be greatly missed by its members. The Food Bank plans to continue to have the land farmed.

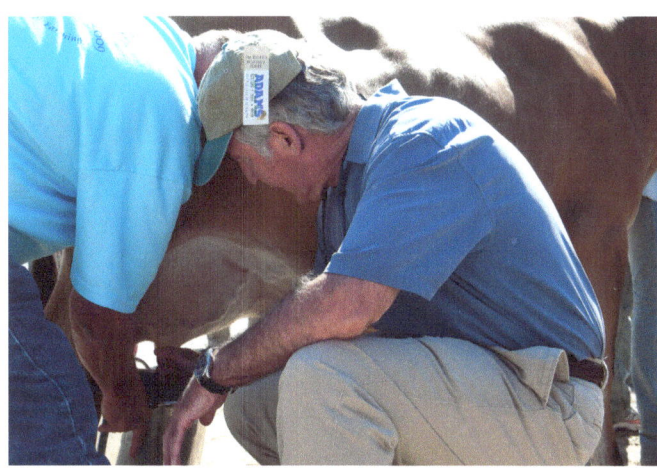

Opposite page, left: Gordon Cook greets the crowd. Opposite page, middle: State Rep. John Scibak reads a citation from the State House of Representatives congratulating the Cooks for their 100th anniversary. Opposite page, right: Mary Thayer addresses the gathering on behalf of the 350th Committee. Top left: U.S. Representative Richard Neal milks a cow at the Cook's 100th Anniversary celebration. Top right: One of the barns at the Cook Farm. Above: The baby cows have lots of visitors.

Top left: Maple sugar candy at the North Hadley Sugar Shack. Top right: Boisvert's corn maze was lots of fun to wander through. Left: The North Hadley Sugar Shack yard is stocked full of fall produce. Above: The store offers its own maple syrup products all year.

The Hadley Food Bank Farm and store.

AUTUMN

Opposite page, top: Fall colored hydrangeas gleam in the sun. Opposite page, below: An old tobacco barn in Hockanum. Top left: The flood marker sign at the Bowles' home in Hockanum. Top right: A view from inside the Hockanum Schoolhouse. Above: The Mt. Holyoke Range from Lawrence Plain Road. Right: Mini pumpkins ready for sale.

AMHERST 250TH PARADE

Hadley was proud to participate in its daughter town's 250th Celebration Parade on September 27th. Hadley town officials, police and fire units, and a Hadley float represented the town. The float had a harvest theme, with produce and decorations provided by the Boisvert Family. Many thanks to the float builders: Joe Boisvert, Gerry Devine, Pete Laurenza, Mark Uchneat, Dave Martula, Kristen Stypeck and Mary and Rick Thayer. The float was pulled by Michael Mushenski. During the parade, Mary, Mark, Pete and Joe handed out mini pumpkins to an appreciative crowd.

Hadley was also represented at Wethersfield's 375th celebration on October 4. Gerry Devine and David Martula carried the Hadley 350th banner in our mother town's parade, followed by Hadley Fire and Police Units.

Clockwise from top left: Hadley's float in the Amherst 250th parade; Joe Boisvert hands out mini pumpkins to an eager crowd; the float ready to start in the parade; putting the float together at Joe Boisvert's farm.

REUNE WITH A TUNE

The Hopkins Alumni Association presented a concert called "Reune with a Tune." Eight very talented local singers performed favorite songs from the '50s and '60s, accompanied expertly by Norinne Jacobus Tiley on the piano. The quality and professionalism of the performance was a delight. There was a lot of laughter from the audience and a few songs were modified to make them uniquely Hadley. The show ended with a rousing standing ovation from the large audience. "Miss Jacobus," as many Hadley residents remember Norinne, who organized the show, was the music director at Hopkins Academy in the 1960s; it was her first job out of college. She was fondly welcomed by her former students in the audience.

Top: Norinne Jacobus Tiley. Above: Reune with a Tune performers and special guest Eddie Forman (at left).

350TH "5K FOR FARMLAND" ROAD RACE

During one of the wettest and coldest days of the fall about 300 hardy people came out to run or walk through Hadley's historic farming area in the Great Meadow. The event was in celebration of Hadley's 350th Anniversary and all proceeds went to helping The Kestrel Trust protect more farmland in the Valley.

Kestrel Trust extends special thanks to: Kohl Construction, Northampton Cooperative Bank, and Whole Foods Market for underwriting the event; Sugarloaf Mountain Athletic Club and Hadley 350th Committee for cosponsoring the event, and especially to Donna Utakis and David Martula for organizing *all* the runner logistics and registration; Wheatberry Cafe, Great Meadow Fruits, and Winter Moon Farm for donating local bread, jam, and carrots and hummus in addition to Whole Foods' yummy treats; all the businesses who donated prizes: Toy Box, Zoar Outdoor, The Healing Zone, Raven Used Books, Loose Goose Cafe, Amherst Family Chiropractic, One Hour Therapeutic Massage, Bart's Cafe, Northampton Coffee, Amherst Coffee, Whisk(e)y Bar, Northampton Running Co., EMS, Hadley Garden Center, Judie's, Daily Hampshire Gazette, and The Leading Edge; the dozens of volunteers who took care of registration, set up, finish line timing, clean up, food, coffee, water, parking, and anything else you could pitch in on; JMPT Quartet for wonderful live music; all the runners and walkers who participated despite the rain and those who pre-paid, but wisely stayed home warm and dry!

THE FIRST CONGREGATIONAL CHURCH OF HADLEY: CELEBRATING 350 YEARS OF WORSHIP AND SERVICE

The First Congregational Church of Hadley was an avid supporter of the Town of Hadley's 350th Anniversary celebration events. In 1659, the founders of the church and town were the same people; there was no separation of church and state. The church proudly offered up the use of its 200 year old building in its age old capacity as the Hadley Meeting House for the town events of Founder's Day, and the Arts Festival.

In 1659, after more than five years of theological disputes within the Churches at Hartford and Wethersfield, Connecticut, a group of "withdrawers" removed themselves from those churches. Representatives of the group had asked Major John Pynchon of Springfield, Massachusetts to purchase the fertile lands on the Connecticut River to the east and north of Northampton, which had been founded in 1654. Together with their pastor, Parson John Russell from the Wethersfield Church, the "withdrawers" established a settlement at Norwottuck which became known as Hadley.

October 18, 2009, was designated by the First Congregational Church of Hadley as a Day of Celebration, commemorating its own 350th year anniversary. The festivities began with a special

Opposite page: The 5K race course through the Great Meadow. (Photo courtesy of the Kestrel Trust) Above: Current and former pastors: The Rev. Leo Hourihan, The Rev. Lorain Giles, The Rev. Sarah Buteux, The Rev. James Ewen, The Rev. Darrell Holland.

350th Anniversary Cake for the First Congregational Church of Hadley.

worship service, Celebrating 350 years of Worship and Service, lead by Reverend Sarah Buteux, in which the sermon focused on the supposition that Reverend John Russell was the true "Angel of Hadley." Reverend Russell was the first pastor of the First Church of Hadley, and a man of tremendous faith and courage, who sacrificed much to extend God's peace and hospitality to two fugitive regicides, hospitality which was reflected by the members of his congregation, and continues in the congregation today. Since Reverend John Russell was so central to Hadley's early days, as he was pastor and a leader of the town for the first 33 years, the sermon is reprinted on the following pages.

The invocation from the anniversary worship service was as follows: *On this day of celebration we come, O Lord, as have the generations before us, to seek your blessing and sing your praise. We give you thanks for the founding families of Hadley who built this church by faith, for the many generations who have sustained this congregation with their love and devotion, and for the members and friends who stand here even now rejoicing in all you have done for us. May our congregation continue to grow in wisdom and compassion and lead with love that we might be a light to those around us. And may your name be praised here, now and evermore. Amen.*

As an extension of hospitality, and of celebration, invitations were extended to the mother, daughter and granddaughter churches of the First Congregational Church of Hadley to join in the days' events as honored guests. Several accepted and attended the event, including a grandmother church, and presented tokens of support during the special service. Also in keeping with the celebration, the service was attended and assisted by several former pastors of First Church, both settled and interim. To complete the spectrum of special visitors, several town officials and others from the community were in attendance.

Following the celebration service was a special luncheon, extending the hospitality of the congregation in the form of food and fellowship which proved very filling. Finger sandwiches and a 350th birthday cake filled the body; making new acquaintances and re-establishing old contacts filled the spirit. Special displays of brief bios of former pastors with photos, as well as photos of church members and activities past, were on display.

A free concert completed the day of celebration. The Pioneer Valley Fiddlers performed for a few hours in the afternoon. Again, the general public was welcome to attend the event, which was a boon for the many fans of the Pioneer Valley Fiddlers. The music itself was light and fun, and the musicians very talented.

Entertaining Angels, Rev. Sarah Buteux October 18, 2009

> "Let mutual love continue. Do not neglect to show hospitality to strangers,
> for by doing so some have entertained angels without knowing it."
> —Hebrews 13: 1–2

I've often said that you can't live in Hadley for long without seeing an angel. I typically see him hanging either in the living room over the couch or in the dining room over the buffet; depending on whose house I'm in. He can also be found downstairs in our fellowship hall just to the left of the thermostat.

For those of you who have no idea what I'm talking about, I'm referring to a painting by Frederick Chapman known as the "Angel of Hadley." If you are new to Hadley and someone (like, say, Fred Oakley or Ken Parker) sees you looking at it, they'll invariably tell you the story of that fateful day, September 1st I believe it was, back in the year 1675, when the townspeople of Hadley were attacked by Native Americans.

According to the story, everyone in town was gathered in the church meetinghouse listening to our first minister, the Rev. John Russell, when all of a sudden they heard a great commotion outside and realized their village was under attack. The men ran out, muskets in hand, but were totally overwhelmed. Until, that is, a man appeared out of nowhere in full army regalia brandishing a sword, his white hair shining in the sun, and marshaled the men into fighting formation. Under his expert command the native attack was repelled, the fires were put out, and the town was saved. But, as the story goes, when the dust cleared the white haired general was nowhere to be found. And so the people concluded that their savior must have been an angel.

It's an awesome story, and as soon as they finish telling it to you, Hadleyites—being the good decent folk that they are—will immediately confess to you that it's not true. At least not the really interesting made-for-TV movie part, because according to historians there is no evidence that Native Americans attacked Hadley on that day at all.

However, you dig around a little more, and you learn that battle or no battle, the white haired general did exist. His name was Goffe. He and his fellow countryman, General Whalley, were on the run from the British Crown for having signed a former king's death warrant. They had fled here to the new world and finally found sanctuary in the way back of beyond; a little settlement on the east side of the river Connecticut called Hadley. And it was no less than the Rev. Russell himself who welcomed these two men and agreed to hide them in a secret room in his house lest they be caught and extradited by agents of the crown.

Now some stories are too good to be true, and some stories are too strange to make up. I can't help but think that the legend of the Angel of Hadley falls somewhere in between. In fact the more I've thought about this, the more I've wondered if maybe the whole scene from Chapman's painting did occur. I just wonder if maybe the good folk of Hadley, having put two and two together, had decided by the day after to keep the whole event on the down low, if you will, and let history play out something a little more like this…

Angel of Hadley: The Cover Up
by Church School Coordinator Lauri Osip

Scene: Rev. Russell's front lawn
[Reverend Russell is hoeing his front garden. He is approached by two men in trench coats.]
Agent 1: Excuse me sir. Are you the Reverend Russell?
Agent 2: The Reverend John Russell?
Rev. Russell: Yes. Yes I am. And who might you be?
Agent 1: I'm Special Agent Brown. And this is my partner, Special Agent Friday. We are agents of the Crown and are investigating a sighting of a dangerous criminal of special interest to the King. Do you have a few moments to answer some questions?
Rev. Russell: Gentlemen, I am situated in the middle of nowhere. What would I know about English criminals?
Agent 2: That wasn't the answer we were looking for. Do you have time to speak here, or do we need to take you with us back to Boston?
Rev. Russell: Calm down, please. I only state the obvious. But if you wish to ask questions, then do so now. I do not have the time or inclination to travel to Boston. My flock needs me here.
[The commotion has drawn the attention of several townsmen, who rally behind the pastor.]
Agent 1: Funny. I've never seen a pastor hoeing weeds.
Mr. Smith: You obviously haven't been to church on Sundays.
Agent 1: And you are?
Mr. Smith: Samuel Smith.
Agent 1: Mr. Smith. What makes you think I don't attend church?
Mr. Smith: What a pastor does is weed the evil out of the hearts of men. Are you even Christian, Sir?
Agent 1: What I am does not matter. I am the one asking questions here. *[Turns to Rev. Russell.]* Reverend, where were you yesterday at approximately 12 noon?
Rev. Russell: I was in the First Church meeting house delivering a clear and inspiring sermon to my parishioners.
Agent 2: And did anything unusual happen during your inspired service?
Rev. Russell: Unusual?
Agent 2: Something like an attack by local savages?
Rev. Russell: Savages?
Mr. Hubbard: I think he's talkin' about those Webster boys. They can be a little rowdy.
Agent 2: I am not speaking of any Websters. I am speaking about Indians.
Mr. Hubbard: Nope. Don't recall any Indians.
Mr. Smith: Me neither.
Agent 1: Perhaps they were defeated by a frightfully bearded man wearing a uniform and bearing a sword?

Angel of Hadley skit performed at the 350th anniversary celebration of the First Congregational Church of Hadley. Left to right: Debbie Ward, Shirley Parsons, Rick Ward, Kurt Betchick, Bob Anderson, Ruth Morse and Toni Wilcox.

Rev. Russell: Where did you hear a story like that?
Agent 1: We have our sources.
Agent 2: Mr. Thomas White is a very reliable source.
Mr. Hubbard: [snort of laughter] Tom White? Ha! He was visitin' yesterday alright, but he slept through the entire sermon.
Mr. Smith: I believe I heard him snoring.
Mrs. Smith: Not to mention the drooling. I had to clean that mess up when he was through.
Agent 2: He said that right in the middle of the fire and brimstone, the door to the meeting house opened and an old soldier appeared, swathed in sunlight, brandishing a sword and claiming Indians were about to attack.
Mr. Hubbard: [snort of laughter] Aw hel….oops, heck! The only way Tom could have seen that was through his eyelids. Must have been some dream!
Mr. Smith: I even heard him mumbling in his sleep.
Mr. Clark: Yeah, something about not wanting to wind up dead or bald.
Mr. Hubbard: What a nightmare. He's not far from the bald status. Poor guy.
Agent 1: Ahem! Mr. White was most explicit in his description of events.
Mr. Hubbard: Must have been a detailed nightmare.
Mr. Smith: That's what happens when you imbibe too much Aqua Vitae before church.
Mr. Clark: Yep. Sermon puts you to sleep. Then the demon in the rum dances in your dreams.

Mr. Hubbard: With all that going on, no wonder White was looking for an angel to save him.
Rev. Russell: Agents, I do not think we can be of any assistance to you. I know my flock very well, and other than Mr. White, who has visited us before, we had no strangers in town yesterday.
Agent 2: Then you wouldn't mind if we just take a look around and talk with your townspeople.
Rev. Russell: Be my guest. You'll be wasting your time. Time better spent on the road to Boston before the rains come.
Agent 1: You predict the weather, as well as save souls.
Rev. Russell: I'm a pastor and a farmer. Judging the climate is in the job description.
Agent 2: Well, we'll just be wandering around if you recall anything more about yesterday's incident. Let me just say it will work in your favor if you volunteer the information than if we find out from other sources. At that point is could go very badly for you.
Mrs. Smith: [huge audible gasp] You would threaten a man of God? What kind of man are you?
Agent 2: Like the reverend says, it's in the job description. Good day.
[The agents slowly meander away.]
Rev. Russell: Good folks of Hadley. Thank you for your support. There is nothing more to see here, so let us all get back to work.
[Two ladies move off toward stage right.]
Mrs. Dickinson: [to Mrs. Smith] Do you think something bad will happen to Reverend Russell?
Mrs. Smith: Nay. God certainly would not send us an angel to lead us into the wilderness, only to let the devil snatch him away. We have only to show God how grateful we are for his gift and remain silent about the rest.
[A reporter comes out from behind a tree.]
Reporter: Good day to you ladies, Mr. Rivera, reporter for the Boston Globe, at your service. I wonder if I might have a moment of your time? You see I'm looking for a story.
Mrs. Dickinson: Something like: it was a dark and stormy night. . . .
Reporter: Not exactly. . . .
Mrs. Smith: [Clearly nervous] How about: it was a bright and sunny morning, and the members of the town were gathered in the meeting house for Sunday service. All was peaceful and quiet until the front doors opened with a bang. And there, standing in the doorway with a halo of light surrounding him, was an angel sent from heaven to deliver his people from certain death.
Reporter: That's it.
Mrs. Dickinson: [Stepping lightly on Mrs. Smith's foot] Never happened.
Reporter: But you just described it all as if you were there.
Mrs. Smith: Never happened.
Reporter: So, what am I supposed to do with the tale you just told. *The Globe* only publishes stories it can verify.
Mrs. Dickinson: I'm sorry sir. Maybe you ought to create your own newspaper. A little tabloid that tells interesting stories not based on facts. You would probably make a mint.
Mrs. Smith: You could call it *The Boston Inquirer*. Or something like that.

Reporter: Not a bad idea. Ladies, thank you for your time. Good day to you.
Mrs. Smith and Mrs. Dickinson: And to you sir.
[As he walks away, both women sigh with relief, and walk off stage.]

Now of course there is no way we can prove that things happened this way or not. Perhaps the historians are right and the whole tale is nothing more than a myth. But when I think of Hadley and the character of its people, I can't help but wonder if maybe General Goffe did make an appearance on that fateful day. Only the people, out of love and concern for their pastor, did everything in their power to cover up the incident lest Rev. Russell find himself in trouble as well.

You know John Russell hid those two men in his house for over ten years, and buried at least one, if not both of them, here in Hadley. There were trusted townsfolk who carried correspondence for those men back and forth to their families in England. I think we all know how hard it is to keep secrets, especially big ones, in a small town, but I think, by virtue of the fact that we live here, we also have the privilege of knowing the lengths people will go to and the risks they will take to care for and protect one another in a small town as well. Thanks be to God that, at least here in Hadley, some things never change.

The way I see it, our town may or may not have been saved by an angel 333 years ago, but I feel quite confident that Generals Whaley and Goffe certainly were in the person of the Rev. Russell. He risked his own life to save theirs; opened his home, shared his food, and preserved the lives of those two men till God called them home. What I want you to remember today is that those who knew of his efforts, and I wouldn't have been surprised if the whole town did by the end, did all in their power to protect their pastor and those two men as well.

Be it myth or history, I think the people of Hadley are heirs to the truth that beats at the heart of this story and that for generation after generation you have remained true to this legacy. It is such a privilege to serve as pastor here in large part because that twin spirit of radical hospitality and unwavering loyalty lives on in all of you.

The writer of Hebrews counsels us to: "Let mutual love continue. Do not neglect to show hospitality to strangers, for by doing so some have entertained angels without knowing it." This is most certainly true. But go forth today remembering that the beauty of hospitality is that it works both ways. Not only do we have the opportunity to entertain angels, but sometimes by extending hospitality to others, we are granted the grace to become like angels as well.

Let us pray: O Lord, I pray that Rev. Russell's spirit and that of our founders would live on in us as we seek to follow you just as they did. Grant us the grace and the courage to go where you lead, to stand by one another even as we stand up to the powers that be when those powers become oppressive. Grant us a measure of their generosity of spirit that we too might be always at the ready to open our church and our homes to all who would seek sanctuary here, and to share of our own resources, just as they did, with those in need. Our history begins with the work of many angels, may we continue their work in kind till your kingdom come and your will is done here on earth as it is in heaven. Amen

ANGELS OF HADLEY PLAY

The Hadley 350th History Fair Weekend took place on Friday, October 23, through Sunday October 25, 2009. The weekend began with the opening of the *Angels of Hadley* original play, featuring the Hopkins Academy Drama Club. The play was also performed on Saturday evening and Sunday afternoon. The playwright, Brian Marsh, is a descendant of several Hadley founding families. The play was directed by Irene Thornton and Brian Marsh. The stage manager was Nathaniel Mathews, original music by Mitch Chakour, sound design by Darrell McTaque, and lighting design by Pat Serio. The play's leading parts were filled by John Tyler, Kristin Szymkowicz, Marisa Babb and Tripp Aquadro. Brian West, Gerry Devine (two current selectmen) and James Maksimoski (current Planning Board Chairman) had small speaking parts, to the delight of the audience. *Angels of Hadley* was a very special contribution to the 350th celebration. It has been preserved both as a DVD and in a photo book.

Clockwise from top left: Kristin Szymkowicz and Marisa Babb perform; Marisa Babb in the glacier dance; Fred Goodhue as William Goffe.

Playwright, director and actor Brian Marsh.

"One of the joys of being playwright is writing to the truth of a situation. Truth, from the playwright's perspective, has less to do with fact and far more to do with a certain creative or spiritual understanding. That is what *Angels of Hadley* is all about; it is a creative approach to the truth that comes from a certain understanding of this place in which we live and work. Such truth doesn't come so much from scholarship or research, although these have certainly informed our work. Rather, it comes more from a particular engagement between the people and the land in which they have lived. The landscape works on us; it changes us; Hadley has formed us more than we have changed this place."

—Brian Marsh, *Director and Playwright*

Top left: John Tyler guides the audience through the play. Above: Actors form the seven sisters of the Mt. Holyoke range. Below left: Cast members, left to right, Aaron Graham-Horowitz, Marisa Babb, Izabela Czarnieck, John Tyler, Kristen Szymkowicz, Emma Hudgik, Christina Kazalis, Ian Fox, and Jessica Krause. Below right: Brian West, Gerry Devine and James Maksimoski.

THE HISTORY FAIR

The Saturday events began with living history displays and demonstrations on the West Street Common that lasted through the day. This included Benjamin Church's Recreated Company performing firing drills, The Society of the 17th Century performing 17th Century crafts and games, and three Native American re-enactors, Ken Hamilton from Maine, John Santos from Northampton, and Tom Turck from Malden, Massachusetts. The weather was a constant drizzle but the events went on as scheduled.

At noontime, a proclamation was read by State Representative John Scibak on the West Street Common declaring October 24, 2009, Clarence Hawkes Day. Jim Freeman—who wrote a book on Clarence Hawkes that was published in 2009, and also contributed an essay on Clarence Hawkes for the book *Cultivating a Past: Essays on the History of Hadley, Massachusetts*—arranged this event and accepted the proclamation for the town.

The history fair included four lectures, covering a variety of topics. All the lectures were very well attended.

The first was a talk and tour of the 1840 Hockanum Schoolhouse on Route 47 South. Mary Thayer led the talk, and former students Marge Barstow and Charlie Johnson shared childhood memories of attending the school. This was the first event at the schoolhouse following major renovations that were funded by the town and the Community Preservation Act.

Next was a lecture given by Jeffrey Mish (Hopkins Academy Class of 2003) in the Museum room on the second floor of the Goodwin Memorial Library. Jeffrey spoke about the Eastern Europeans in the area and showed a video he put together in 2005 interviewing many local Eastern European people both young and old.

The third lecture was given by Allan Zuchowski at the Porter Phelps Huntington House Barn at 130 River Drive. Allan's talk was on the history of the Native Americans in the area. He spoke to an overflowing crowd.

The last lecture of the day was given by Dr. Joseph Zgrodnik, at the North Hadley Hall. Dr. Zgrodnik spoke about attending both the North Hadley School, and North Hadley Roman Catholic Church in the North Hadley Hall in the 1950s. He also had former students and church goers speak about their experiences. Bob Hahn spoke at length about his experiences in the North Hadley School.

The Goodwin Memorial Library played historical children's games and displayed models of some of Hadley's old homes that were made by Hopkins Academy's eighth graders for a science project in the Spring of 2009.

The Hadley Historical Society hosted an Open House at the Museum Room located on the second floor of the Goodwin Memorial Library. There were mannequins on display dressed in vintage clothing. In addition, three Trustees of the Historical Society modeled clothing from the late 19th and early 20th centuries. Ellie Niedbala, a teacher at Hooker School for 32 years, modeled an early 1900 bathing suit; Diane Baj, a lifetime resident of Hadley, modeled an early 1900

Left: Joe Zgrodnik gives a talk at the North Hadley Hall. Right: Old photos are on display at the Most Holy Redeemer Church's breakfast. (Photo by MaryAnn Mish)

gym suit; and Peg Miller, a resident of Hadley for 45 years, modeled a dress possibly worn by a woman in the late 1800s or early 1900s as she went about her daily chores. (Both Ellie and Diane participated in Hadley's 300th anniversary parade in 1959; Ellie was on the "Angel of Hadley" float and Diane was a majorette in the Hopkins Academy band.) Also on display was clothing, both children's and adult's, from different periods. All of the clothing had been donated by Hadley residents over the years.

Some of the people in attendance had come from distant places and took advantage of the Society's genealogy files to research ancestors who had made their homes in Hadley. The Open House was a huge success and was attended by about 75 to 80 interested persons, in spite of the inclement weather.

The First Congregational Church had a delicious fall harvest supper with chicken-n-gravy, biscuits, potatoes, and pie.

On Sunday morning, the sun finally shone, and the Most Holy Redeemer Church had a coffee hour and displays of old photos from the former St. John's and Holy Rosary Churches.

On Sunday afternoon, a book signing for the book *Cultivating a Past: Essays on the History of Hadley, Massachusetts* took place at Barnes and Noble.

The weekend closed with a concert at the North Hadley Congregational Church "Songs of Inspiration," featuring "The Creation: A Rock Contata," The North Hadley Congregational Church Choir, and friends.

Opposite page: Native American re-enactor Ken Hamilton. Clockwise from above left: Hockanum Schoolhouse; firing drills by the Benjamin Church's Recreated Company; a member of The Society of the 17th Century demonstrates early crafts.

Top left and above left: Demonstrations on the Common. Top right: Hadley Historical Society members Peg Miller, Diane Baj and Ellie Niedbala model vintage clothing. Above right: State Rep. John Scibak presents the Clarence Hawkes Day Proclamation to James Freeman. Opposite page: Governor Deval Patrick's proclamation that October 24, 2009 is Clarence Hawkes Day.

Commonwealth of Massachusetts

A Proclamation

His Excellency Governor Deval L. Patrick

Whereas Clarence Hawkes is celebrated today as a great and prolific American author who penned nearly sixty published novels and essays as well as produced volumes of highly acclaimed poetry; and

Whereas He overcame great hardship in his youth after suffering the loss of his eyesight, as well as part of one leg, to then graduate from the Perkins School for the Blind as a classmate and friend of Helen Keller; and

Whereas Hawkes received great praise from both the general public and renowned naturalists, including President Theodore Roosevelt, for the depth and accuracy of his writings on the natural world and American wildlife, including such titles as *"Shovellhorns, the Biography of a Moose"*, *"Master Frisky"* and *"Jungle Joe, Pride of the Circus; the Story of a Trick Elephant"*; and

Whereas Recognized internationally, his works appear in French, Japanese, German, Danish and Chinese, as well as in Braille; and

Whereas Clarence Hawkes' storytelling ability, in addition to the fidelity he displayed when personifying and portraying his animal subjects, was also recognized by Amherst College, Hobart College, Syracuse University and American International College, as the recipient of honorary degrees from each institution; and

Whereas Clarence Hawkes contributed greatly to the civic life of Hadley, Massachusetts, designing twenty floats for the community's Bicentennial Celebration and composing the anthem for the local high school, Hopkins Academy,

Now, Therefore, I, Deval L. Patrick, Governor of the Commonwealth of Massachusetts, do hereby proclaim October 24th, 2009 to be,

CLARENCE HAWKES DAY

And urge all the citizens of the Commonwealth to take cognizance of this event and participate fittingly in its observance.

Given at the Executive Chamber in Boston, this first day of October, in the year two thousand and nine, and of the Independence of the United States of America, the two hundred and thirty-third.

By His Excellency

DEVAL L. PATRICK
GOVERNOR OF THE COMMONWEALTH

WILLIAM FRANCIS GALVIN
SECRETARY OF THE COMMONWEALTH

God Save the Commonwealth of Massachusetts

"350 X 24" HADLEY ARTISTS ON EXHIBIT

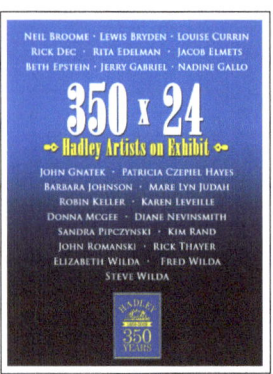

The third and final art event, "350 x 24," was held during the months of November and December at the U.S. Fish & Wildlife Gallery building. It was coordinated by John Romanski and Jane Nevinsmith. Steve and Elizabeth Wilda designed the announcement card and poster. The hanging of the artwork was done by Nancy Fernald, Rita Edelman, John Romanski and Steve Wilda. Remarkably, twenty-four Hadley artists participated in displaying their artwork. Never before had there been such a large congregation of talented Hadley artists for one exhibition. Jane Nevinsmith organized the reception, which was held on November 7th, and was very well attended by the public.

The art events were funded by the Hadley 350th Committee. All of the artists and the community are grateful for the financial support and publicity given to the visual arts by Hadley's 350th Committee.

Artists and viewers at the opening reception of the "350 x 24" art exhibit at the U.S. Fish & Wildlife Gallery.

"350 x 24" Hadley artists on Exhibit

Neil Broome, Lewis Bryden, Louise Currin, Rick Dec, Rita Edelman, Jacob Elmets, Beth Epstein, Jerry Gabriel, Nadine Gallo, John Gnatek, Patricia Czepiel Hayes, Barbara Johnson, Mare Lyn Judah, Robin Keller, Karen Leveille, Donna McGee, Diane Nevinsmith, Sandra Pipczynski, Kim Rand, John Romanski, Rick Thayer, Elizabeth Wilda, Fred Wilda and Steve Wilda

Above: Hadley artists at the opening reception for "350 x 24," front row, left to right, Neil Broome, Barbara Johnson, Rita Edelman, Diane Nevinsmith, Louise Currin, Mare Lyn Judah; second row, left to right, John Gnatek, Fred Wilda, Donna McGee, Elizabeth Wilda, Steve Wilda; back row, John Romanski, Sandra Pipczynski and Rick Thayer. (Photo by Oscar Edelman) At left: Paintings by Neil Broome.

NEW "WELCOME TO HADLEY" SIGN

A project to install a Welcome to Hadley sign on Route 9 at the intersection of Route 9 and Cross Path Road came to fruition on a bright and sunny day in January, 2010. Donations to make the sign possible came from several local individuals and businesses. The Hadley 350th Committee was the main sponsor. Hadley residents Betsy Alden and Debbie Windoloski spearheaded the project and plan to install solar lighting and plantings in the spring. The sign was created and installed by Design Works, a New Jersey–based firm.

Left to right: Rick and Mary Thayer, Sign maker Larry Plummer, Gerry Devine, Betsy Alden, Mark Reed, Bill Drozdal, Sandi and Wayne Buckhout stand in front of the newly installed welcome sign.

DEDICATION OF THE RUSSELL PLAQUES

The Hadley 350th Committee, working with Fred Oakley of the Cemetery Committee, had two 16" x 10" bronze plaques made. The plaques display the inscriptions from the gravestones of the Rev. John Russell and his wife. After years of exposure to the elements, the Russells' tabletop gravestones in the Old Hadley Cemetery are no longer legible. The new plaques were installed near each gravestone mounted on granite bases. Gerry Devine welcomed the gathering and Mary Thayer gave a short introduction telling about Rev. John and Rebekah Russell, and the Rev. Sarah Buteux of the First Congregational Church wrote a prayer read by Deacon Lisa West.

The Rev. John Russell is a key figure in Hadley's history. He graduated from Harvard University in 1645, one of the first graduates of the new college. He led the group of families from Wethersfield, Hartford and Windsor who founded Hadley in 1659. Rev. Russell served as both the pastor of Hadley's church for 33 years, from 1659 to 1692, and as a leader of the new town. He is remembered for hiding the regicides, General William Goffe and General Edward Whalley, in his home for over twelve years. He was also a strong advocate for the fledgling Hopkins School, which later became Hopkins Academy. His wife, Rebekah, died in 1688. Her stone is the oldest gravestone in Hadley's cemeteries.

Rev. Russell's grave site is a popular destination for those researching Hadley's early days. The 350th Committee is pleased to support this effort and to honor Hadley's founders.

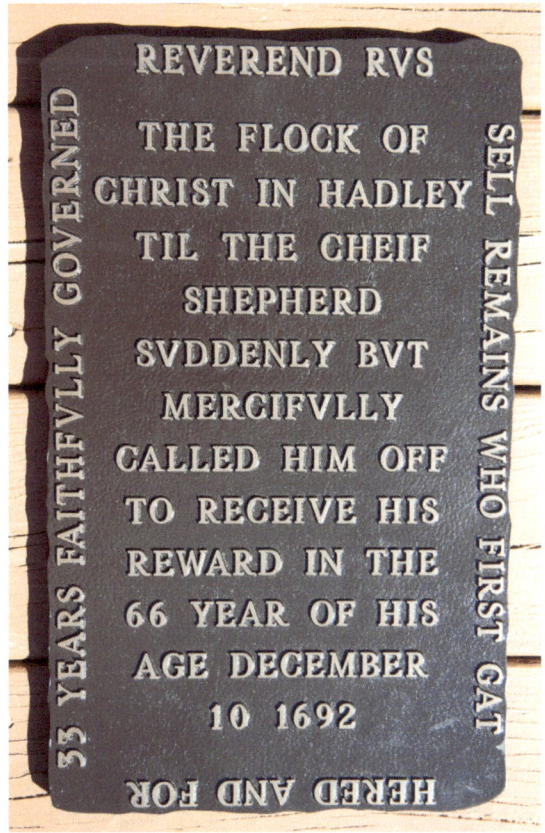
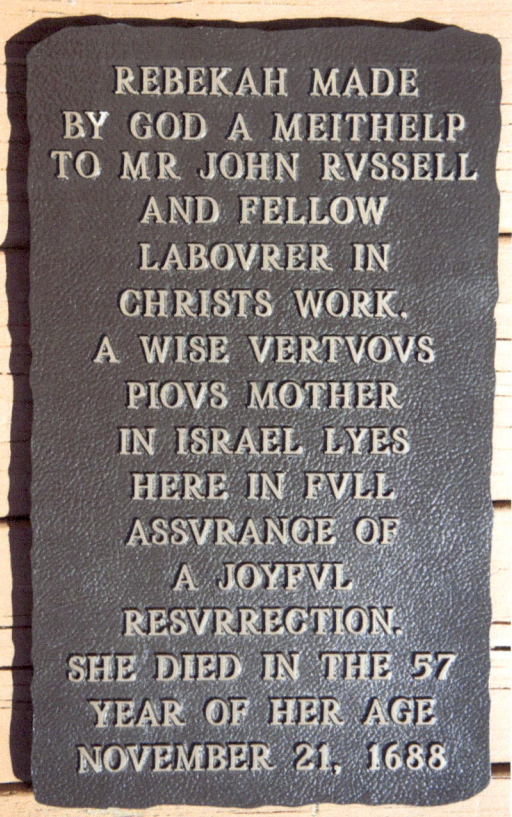

THE WHITE HOUSE

WASHINGTON

December 29, 2009

I am pleased to join all those celebrating the 350th anniversary of the Town of Hadley, Massachusetts. Such a momentous occasion is an opportunity to reflect on the history of your community and the people who made it what it is today.

Your community's story begins before Thomas Jefferson penned the Declaration of Independence and George Washington took the first Oath of Office. During your journey, we struggled through a Civil War and thrived during industrialization. We endured the Great Depression and two World Wars, drew inspiration from Dr. King's dream, and watched Neil Armstrong land on the moon. Since our Nation's founding, our country has evolved through times of trial and triumph. Together, as family, friends, and neighbors, you have written your own chapter in the narrative of the United States.

Today, as we work to fulfill America's promise, we look to our past for lessons on courage and determination. As we continue our journey, I hope you are inspired by the principles upon which our Nation was founded, and by the hard work and sacrifice of our forebears.

Congratulations on this special milestone.

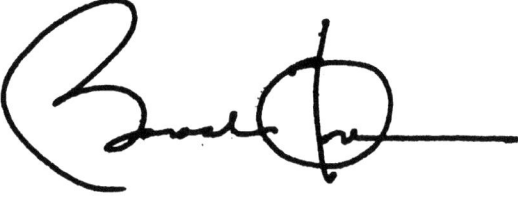

United States Senate
WASHINGTON, DC 20510-2102

JOHN KERRY
MASSACHUSETTS

COMMITTEES:
COMMERCE, SCIENCE, AND TRANSPORTATION
FINANCE
FOREIGN RELATIONS
SMALL BUSINESS

One Bowdoin Square
Tenth Floor
Boston, MA 02114

June 13, 2009

Dear Friends,

    I am delighted to offer my best wishes to all in Hadley on the occasion of the 350th anniversary of your town's founding. The history of Hadley and the story of its settlement is one of remarkable personal courage on the part of its founders and first inhabitants, a fierce independence of spirit made all the more remarkable for its devotion to the common and greater good. These same characteristics are as obvious today in Hadley as they were in 1659.

    In large part thanks to Hadley's first families' risk-taking, Massachusetts was able to flourish economically and secure its place as an early power during our nation's youth. Hadley, though perhaps small in the eyes of some, played an enormous role in our Commonwealth's history and America's founding and deserves a special place in our history. The entrepreneurial spirit and extraordinary work ethic of Hadley's early inhabitants allowed the town's agricultural and commercial industry to flourish, establishing Hadley as one of America's first global exporter.

    I salute everyone in Hadley today on the 350th anniversary of your Town's founding and wish you an even more remarkable next 350 years.

Sincerely,

John F. Kerry

John F. Kerry
United States Senator

HOUSE OF REPRESENTATIVES
WASHINGTON, D.C. 20515

RICHARD E. NEAL
SECOND DISTRICT
MASSACHUSETTS

April 2, 2010

When Rev. John Russell founded Hadley in 1659 I'm sure he could have only hoped to see his town prosper and develop into what it is today. The celebration of 350 years as a town is truly remarkable. I am proud to have been part of this wonderful year in Hadley's history. From the commemoration of Founder's Day, to the grand 350th parade, the 350th Committee has captured the vast and important history of Hadley. The events of this year will not soon be forgotten by any of those involved. The fourth of July fireworks were a sight to behold, as were the many historic displays presented across town over the past year.

As this memorable year draws to an end, I would like to express my sincere gratitude to all of the thousands of volunteers who made this year's celebrations so successful. The way in which this community has come together around a common cause is inspiring. I am proud to represent Hadley in the United States House of Representatives.

Sincerely,

Richard E. Neal
House of Representatives

COMMONWEALTH OF MASSACHUSETTS
MASSACHUSETTS SENATE
STATE HOUSE, BOSTON 02133-1053

Senator Stan Rosenberg, President Pro Tem　　　　　　　　　District Office
Hampshire and Franklin District　　　　　　　　　　　　　　1 Prince St.
Room 320　　　　　　　　　　　　　　　　　　　　　　　　Northampton, MA 01060
617.722.1532　　　　　　　　　　　　　　　　　　　　　　413.584.1649
Fax: 617.722.1062　　　　　　　　　　　　　　　　　　　　Fax:
413.582.0113

Stan.Rosenberg@state.ma.us

December 8, 2009

To the Citizens of Hadley:

Congratulations on the 350th anniversary celebration!

It was my distinct pleasure to participate in a number of activities during this celebratory year. I know that many of you devoted a great deal of time and effort to make this year-long celebration a great success. You have carried on the fine traditions that started centuries ago and have demonstrated, through your dedication to service, that Hadley is more than a place on the map, and that this anniversary is more than a moment in time. I hope that everyone who has ever called Hadley "home" will take great pride in this accomplishment.

Everyday I encounter people who are rediscovering the power of community service, of pitching in to help others and of showing our children the importance of good citizenship. I like to think that people like you are at least partly responsible for this renaissance. I also like to think that the quality of our common future lies in the hands of people who care. If that is truly the case, then the future of the town of Hadley is in excellent hands.

Once again, congratulations. The next 350 years are off to a terrific start!

Sincerely,

Stan Rosenberg

STAN ROSENBERG
State Senator

The Commonwealth of Massachusetts
HOUSE OF REPRESENTATIVES
STATE HOUSE, BOSTON 02133-1054

JOHN W. SCIBAK
REPRESENTATIVE
SECOND HAMPSHIRE DISTRICT
EASTHAMPTON · HADLEY · SOUTH HADLEY

ROOM 42, STATE HOUSE
TEL (617) 722-2370
FAX (617) 722-2215
John.Scibak@hou.state.ma.us

Committees
Vice Chair, Economic Development and Emerging Technologies

DISTRICT OFFICE
TEL (413) 539-6566

January 1, 2010

Hadley 350th Committee
P.O. Box 294
Hadley, MA 01035

Dear Members of the 350th Committee Residents of Hadley:

On this New Years Day, it is fitting to both look back on the past year and to look ahead to the future.

For the Town of Hadley, 2009 will be a year that will not soon be forgotten. From the Dinner Dance in January to the Holiday Sing-a-long in December, Hadley celebrated its history through a series of educational programs, musical and cultural events, local tours, children's activities, and the 350th Celebration Parade.

This was a true community celebration, and I offer my congratulations and thanks to the Hadley 350th Anniversary Committee and the many volunteers for the countless hours spent in planning and preparation over the past year, and to the people of Hadley whose attendance made these events such a great success. Whether attending most of the events or only one or two, one came away with a greater appreciation for the Town of Hadley, its heritage and beauty, the people who live here, and the role that Hadley plays in contributing to the quality of life in the Pioneer Valley.

Now that the Souvenir Shoppe is closed and Hadley settles in to its 351st year, I can't help but think ahead and wonder how the Town will celebrate its 400th Anniversary. While we don't know what Hadley will look like in 2059 and how the community will have changed, we do know that the Hadley 400th Anniversary Committee will have a long way to go in order to match what occurred in 2009.

Once again, thank you and congratulations to the Town of Hadley on your 350th Anniversary.

Sincerely,

John W. Scibak
State Representative

Board of Selectmen
TOWN OF HADLEY

100 Middle Street • Hadley, MA 01035

Telephone (413) 586-0221
Fax (413) 586-5661

To the Hadley 350th Anniversary Committee:

The Board of Selectmen of the Town of Hadley congratulates you on your outstanding achievement that you all worked so hard to bring into being and that you sustained throughout Hadley's anniversary year.

Celebrating Hadley's 350th anniversary took the form of many events. The Gala Ball kicked off the year-long festivities, and its broad community support immediately set the tone for the rest of the year. Founder's Day was successful and brought attention to Hadley's historical and genealogical significance. The parade demonstrated the community's appreciation for the quality of life we enjoy and the kind of civic pride the town takes in its heritage. Then there were the many lectures, concerts, events, publications, and dances that helped round out the year and helped showcase Hadley from many different perspectives and drew in many different audiences.

None of these events would be possible without thousands of hours from volunteers. Many years of planning and preparation went into making the year so successful. Although many people did not receive or want public recognition, the town is grateful for their generous contributions of time, energy, talent, and resources.

We, the Board of Selectmen of the Town of Hadley, Massachusetts, on behalf of the inhabitants, congratulate you on your many contributions to the Town of Hadley. Your achievements serve as an example to others, and we take great satisfaction that you have dedicated yourself to this important and constructive project.

Given this fifteenth day of February in the year two thousand and ten.

_____
Joyce A. Chunglo

_____
Gerald T. Devine

_____
Brian C. West

_____
Daniel Dudkiewicz

_____
Gloria A. DiFulvio
Members, Board of Selectmen

SPECIAL THANK YOUS

Thousands of people helped out during the year. Several newcomers said they now felt so much more a part of the community after volunteering for one of the 350th events or committees. There are so many people to thank, from all those who chaired committees, worked on committees, volunteered for specific events, participated by coming to events or contributed financially. We have tried to thank everyone in this book. We would also like to thank the following, whose dedication, skills and generosity greatly enhanced our celebration.

Rick Thayer

The 350th website, www.hadley350.org, was key to our communication efforts. The website included a complete list of all the events, and pictures, and write-ups after many of the events. There were monthly themes that corresponded to the 350th calendar, pictures of the souvenir items, lists of sponsors and volunteers, and forms needed for some of the events. People both near and far enjoyed keeping up to date on the 350th celebration through the website. A huge thank you to Rick for making the website professional, up-to-date and complete. And thanks for taking wonderful photos throughout the year, many of which are in this book, and for helping out in countless other ways.

Paul Benjamin and Marian Chapman, *The Benjamin Company*

Paul and Marian volunteered to help with our design needs early on. They designed the 350th logo, the 2009 Calendar, the 350th Brochure, the Parade logo, the Parade Souvenir Guide, flyers, posters, ads and more. Their creativity and talents brought these items to a whole new level and greatly enhanced our celebration.

Town of Hadley Employees

The support from the town employees was felt in so many ways, from the Select Board's office being willing to answer so many questions both from the 350th volunteers and the community, the treasurer's and accountant's offices for their fine work keeping track of our income and expenses, the town clerk's office for answering many questions, the Select Board for their incredible support and advice, the Department of Public Works for help with events, especially the parade, for the fire department and police department for being so cooperative and helping out, especially for the parade, for the schools encouraging the students to participate in the 350th celebration, and more.

Andy Morris-Friedman

Andy helped videotape several events, and his films have been shown on TV-5. His efforts have helped preserve 350th events and lectures, to be enjoyed for years to come.

Walter Raphael Mantani

Walter, coordinator of local access channel TV-5, helped videotape many of the events and activities during the year, interviewing spectators and participants alike. Walter also listed 350th announcements and events on TV-5, and he showed 350th and historical films of Hadley weekly.

Pat Serio
Pat videotaped many of the year's events, and put together the video for the 350th parade and the *Angels of Hadley* play, which have been enjoyed by hundreds of people.

Brian Marsh
Brian created an incredible, original play for Hadley, capturing much of the spirit of our town, the flow of time through the centuries, and the connection we have with those who lived here before us. Brian wrote the play, working with the Play Committee while being very receptive to their suggestions. He became even more involved when he assumed the role of director. Brian co-directed the play with Irene Thornton and had an acting part in the play. Brian gave the Town of Hadley a wonderful gift through his words, work and talent. To top it off, it is wonderful to know that Brian is descended from several of Hadley's founders.

Patricia Nobre
Patricia, a graphic designer and graduate student at the University of Massachusetts, designed the beautiful series of booklets on topics in Hadley history (*Hadley in the Civil War* by Eric Freeman, *Pride of All Citizens, Hadley's Town Common and Great Meadow, The Angel of Hadley* by James Freeman, *The Cemeteries and Gravestones of Hadley, Massachusetts*, and more) that will provide an ongoing contribution to local history for many years to come. Patricia went beyond the call of duty to design a very attractive series of publications, and kindly accepted a seemingly-endless number of last-minute suggestions and revisions as each project made its way through toward publication.

Linda Roghaar, *White River Press*
Linda provided ample assistance in bringing a number of projects to fruition, including not only the booklet series and this commemorative book, but also James Freeman's anniversary-year study of Clarence Hawkes. Linda was unfailingly generous with her knowledge, time, and contacts to others in the field, and we benefited greatly from her experience and good will.

Rebecca Neimark, *Twenty-Six Letters*
Rebecca, a book designer, worked with the editors of this 350th commemorative book. Rebecca has been a joy to work with: very professional and talented, and able to keep to a tight schedule and still do an incredible job. Her talents and creativity transformed many pages of text and a multitude of photos into this beautiful book.

The following helped us tremendously by selling 350th DVDs and publications for us, making it easier for people to purchase them: The Goodwin Memorial Library, Barstow's Dairy Store, North Hadley Sugar Shack, the Hadley branch of the Easthampton Savings Bank and the Cat's Cradle.

SPONSORS

The Hadley 350th Committee would like to thank all of the contributors for making this anniversary a truly memorable celebration for the wonderful town of Hadley.

Diamond
Florence Savings Bank

Platinum
Easthampton Savings Bank
Peoples Bank

Gold
Kate Nugent

Silver
TD Bank
Trustees of Hopkins Academy

Bronze
Marjorie Barstow
Berkshire Gas
Cedar Reach Farm
Cowls Building Supply
Devine Overhead Doors
Virginia & Daniel Dudkiewicz
Esselon Café
Four Seasons Wine & Liquor
Margaret & James Freeman
Goulet Trucking, Inc.
Hadley Garden Center
Hadley Hist. Commission
Hadley Lion's Club
Hadley Mother's Club
The Hahn Family
Sara Hills
Karl's Site Work, Inc.
Liquors 44
Tod & Judith Loebel
David & Tanyss Martula
David & Camela Moskin
Moss Nutrition
Most Holy Redeemer Catholic Church
Michael & Robin Murphy
North Hadley Sugar Shack
Polish American Citizens Club

RCI Electric
Stop & Shop (Ahold Financial Services)
Sunbridge Care & Rehabilitation for Hadley at Elaine Manor
Rick & Mary Thayer
UMass Five College Federal Credit Union
Jane Underwood & Alice Underwood
Valley Vodka
Valley Dentists
Alan & Rosalie Weinberg
Western Mass Electric Company
Whole Foods
Zaskey Farm

Donations
Chet Abel & Janet Scott
Joyce & Robert Abel
Acme Automotive Center, Inc.
Aegis Chiropractic & Physical Therapy
Robert & Mary Ellen Ahearn
Bill & Jacqueline Ahlemeyer
Albano and Szumowski, P.C.
Jeffrey & Lorraine Aldrich
All States Asphalt
Amherst Appraisal
Amherst Farmers Supply
Jeanne Ammon
Andrew Paddock Insurance Agency
Arizona Pizza of Hadley
Stephen Armstrong
David Artzerounian
Astarte Farm
Atkins Fruit Bowl, Inc.
Back Nine Advantage
Diane Baj
Helen Baj
Stephen Baj

Lawrence & Kathy Bame
Carl & Lillian Banas
Bank of Western Mass
Lily Barak
Richard & Bernice Baranowski
David & Paula Barstow
Barstow's Longview Farm
Barstow Plumbing & Heating
Baystate Window and Door
Bean Management, LLC -Midas
Robert Belado
Raymond Bender & Mary Pelic
The Benjamin Company
Kenneth Berestka
Orene & Elmer Berg
Berkshire Children and Families
Paul & Joyce Bertrand
Rita Bishko
Jake Bishop
Debora Blodgett
Bobcat of Greater Springfield
Martha & John Boisvert
Pamela Bombardier
Carol Booker
Roberta Boulanger
Cecelia & Stephen Bristol
Lora & David Brown
Marilyn Brown
Norman Brown
Stanley Brown
Stanley and Elizabeth Brown
Kimberly Budd
Cynthia Hahn Caldwell
Kenneth & Kim Carter
Ce-Vail/Bernardston
Carmelina's at the Commons
Ronald and Mary Beth Chevalier
Leona & Richard Chmura
Maria & Richard Coach
Beth Cook & Debra Cook
Complete Disposal

Country Nissan
Courtyard by Marriott
Alan & Nancy Crossley
Curtain Shop
Cumberland Farms
E & H Czelusniak
Dave's Soda & Pet City
Alexandra & James Dawson
Susan & Gerald Delisle
Andree Demay & Suzzy Morin
Devine Farms, Inc.
Devon Lane Farm Supply, Inc.
Dion Tack
Donald Dion
Dowd Insurance
Bertille Dragon
Dwyer & Sanderson
Theodore & Lynne Dziok
Kenneth & Mary-Lelia Earle
Linda Harris & Alan Eccleston
Ecuador Andino Store
David Elvin
Trista & Edward Fedor
Joyce & David Fill
Kathleen Fil
Linda and Hank Fil
Stanley Fil
Thomas Fil
Dr. Katherine Fite
Mary Fitzgibbon
Foodscapes, Inc.
Dorothy Fradera
Susan & Michael Frazier
Dina Friedman & Shel Horowitz
Elizabeth & Richard Fydenkevez
Ernest & Nadine Gallo
Maria Gallo
Maryann Garrahan
Gauthier West
Gail & Brian Glazier
David & Andrea Goguen
Comm. to Re-elect Garvey
Virginia Goldsbury
Nancy Goodman

Denise Gosselin
Ralph & Jennifer Gould
Jean Gowdy
Madelyn & Mike Grala
Fred & Millicent Guerrin
Phillip Gullion & Li-Ann Kuan
Linda Gwozdz
Hadley Fence
Hadley Mother's Club
Patricia & Douglas Hahn
Cathy & Jonathan Campbell Hahn
Joyce & David Hahn
Christopher & Jennifer Hahn
Harold L. Eaton Assoc., Inc.
Lori Harper
John & Anne Hanieski
Deborah Hanlon
Carolyn Hayes & Karyn Kijak
Frederick Hess, DVM
Hillside Organic Pizza, Inc.
Alice Holmes
Hopkins Alumni Association
Kim Hughes
Ideal Movers
Kate Iles
Inspirit Common LLC
Jane's Spa
Java Hut
Jekanowski Farm
Pamela Juengling
Jones Group
Theodore & Helen Kapinos
Keats, Inc.
Kevin & Lisa Kelley
Daniel Kelley
William & Mary-Beth Kennedy
Ken's Catering
James & Cynthia Kicza
Kieras Oil
Mary Fil Kirk
Klepacki and Brookes, DMD
Mark Klepacki
Heather & Michael Klesch
Kim Orinetal Market & Restaurant

Dorothy Kneeland
Cynthia Kochan
Donna Jackson Kohlin
Pauline Kokoski
Stanley & Beverly Kokoski
Dave & Joan Koloski
John & Phyllis Koloski
Julia & John Koloski
Chester & Margaret Konieczny
Andy Korenewsky
David & Joan Koloski
Julie & David Koloski
Angelina & Stanley Kosloski
Margaret Kosloski
Anthony & Carol Kostek
Richard & Carol Kostek
Stephen & Regina Kotfila
Agnes Krzanowski
Linda Laduc
Sim Pheah Lam
Ida Lauter
Robert & Nancy Leveille
Deborah Levenson & Pgennig Margus
John Lipski
Michel Locher
Claire Madej
A.M. Mailhot
Mapleline Farm
Mapleline Farm Home Delivery
Elizabeth & Patrick March
Nancy Markert
Jane Marshall
Mark Marshall & Helen Leung
Mitch's Marina
Patricia McGarry
Melinda McIntosh
James & Lynn McKenna
Sheena McLanahan
William & Jackie Mellen
Mi Terra Mexican Restaurant
Constance Mieczkowski
Owen & Eun Jeong Moniff
Sarah Morin & Andree Demay

Most Holy Redeemer Church Club	Peter & Natalie Root	Virginia Traub
Arthur & Jean Mundt	The Rosenberg Committee	Brenda Tudryn
Murphy McCoubrey	Jeffrey Rothenberg	Kathleen Tudryn
Nature's Finest Creations	Stanley & Stacia Rotkiewicz	Tom Turck
Tim and Teri Neyhart	Marian Roy	United Bank
Norm's Auto Body	Route 9 Diner	Unlimited Business Services
Susan Norris	Irene Russell	George and Dorothy Urch
North Star	James Russell	Elizabeth and Tom Vachula
Kenneth O'Brien	Donald Sabola	Vadar Systems
OESCO, Inc.	Kathleen Miller &	Valley Computerworks
Gary Oleson & Frannie Ness	James Sadlowski	John & Bonnie Vaught
Daniel Omasta	Peter Sadlowski	Robert Vining
Orchard Hill farm Equip., Inc.	Lisa Sanderson	Cynthia Wade
Joseph & Pat Osip	Colleen Murphy Schwerdfeger	John & Mary Walsh
David & Barbara Palangi	Sears	Janet and Walter Wanczyk
Eugene & Anne Palmer	Rep. John W. Scibak	Wanczyk Nursery
Richard J. Palmisano	Jane Sessions Scott	Peter and Marianne Wanczyk
Phyllis & Kenneth Parsons	J.& D. Semensi, Jr.	Maureen Waskiewicz
Shirley Parsons	James Serhant &	Thomas & Carol Waskiewicz
Joan Patriquin	Jane Degenhardt	Ron Welburn
Stephen Peck	Prity Shah & Jon Bete	Kayla Werlin & Wayne
Mary Pelis	Susan & Albert Sheridan	Abercrombie
Katherine Persons	John & Emily Silvestro	Joyce & Arthur West
Mary Ann Phelon	Sirum Equipment Company	Western Mass Endodontics
Pheng Phou	Ellen Snyder & Joellen Smith	Whole Foods
Dennis & Sandra Pipczynski	Edward H. Smola, DMD	Marguerite Wilson
Plainville Farm	Arthur Stern	Sarah Wilson
Edward Pira & Lynn Rule	Sarah Strong	Richard & Jean Yarrows
Polish American Citizens Club	Thomas & Joanne Styspeck	Tom & Mary Yarsley
Barbara & John Pliska	David E. Sullivan	Jerome & Claire Yezierski
Mr. & Mrs. Thomas Quartulli	Sylvan Learning Center	Young Men's Club of Hadley
RJL The Curtain Shop	Syncnicity, Inc.	Ann Zamzow
Katherine Reichert & Marg.	Patricia Szumowski	Carolyn Zawacki
Frerichs	Thomas & Vera Szumowski	Cheng Hui Zheng
Kim Reinier & Paul Alexanderson	Mildred & Donna Szymkowicz	Jacqueline Zuzgo
Mark & Barbara Rejniak	Richard Thayer, Sr	Joan & Thomas Zuzgo
George & Norma Ritter	ThayerCare	Patricia & Thomas Zuzgo
River Drive Auto	Diann & Lee Tolpa	

Thank you to these companies who have donated significant services to the 350th celebration.

American Legion Post 271	Hampshire Hospitality Group	Springfield Republican
Dot Inc Solutions	Home Depot in Hadley	Valley Advocate
FrugalMarketing.com	Kicza Lumber	Young Men's Club of Hadley
Hadley American Legion Post 271	Muddy Brook Farm	WMECO

VOLUNTEERS

Words cannot express our gratitude to all the volunteers that made the 350th celebration possible. So many people came forward willing to lead or lend a hand, and our year-long activities resulted. People helped with what they were passionate about, whether it was history, gardening, painting, farming, dancing or in other areas. The volunteers' pride and love of Hadley was very evident in all that they gave of their time, talents and dedication.

350th Steering Committee
Mary Thayer, Co-Chair
David Martula, Co-Chair
Wayne Buckhout
Sandi Buckhout
Gerry Devine
Betty Fydenkevez
Mary Lou Laurenza
Marla Miller
MaryAnn Mish
Chip Parsons
Kristen Styspeck
John Vassallo
Joyce West

Dinner Dance
Betty Fydenkevez
Carol Zgrodnik
Carol Trane
Camilla World Peace
Mary Thayer
Marianne Wanczyk

Farm Tours
Beth Cook
Paula Barstow

Antique Tractor Show
Bruce Jenks
Tami Kokoski
Paul Ciaglo

Photo Contest
Mary Lou Laurenza
Patsy Lewis
Phyllis Milardo
Allison Ryan
Marcia Wojewoda

350th Road Race
David Martula, Chair
Donna Utakis, Race Director
Sugarloaf Mountain Athletic Club
Kristin DeBoer
The Kestrel Trust

EFO Celebrates Hadley's 350th
Mary Lou Laurenza
Carol Forman
Brenda Pelissier
Elaine Tudryn
Katie Egan

Parade
Chip Parsons, Co-Chair
Norm Barstow, Co-Chair
Janet Barstow
David and Joyce Fill
Carla Grabiec
Chris Hopkins
Dennis Hukowicz
Alan Jacque
John Kieras
John Koloski
Shari Parsons
Jessica and Michael Spanknebel
Holly Zamzow

Parade Volunteers
Thousands of people helped build floats, participated in the parade, or volunteered on parade day. We are very grateful.

Garden and Artist Tours, Artist Festival
Debbie Windoloski
Steve Wilda
Elizabeth Wilda
Mary Thayer
Nancy Fernald

Fireman's Muster and Block Party
Ken Rodak
Mary Lou Laurenza

History Fair, Angels of Hadley Play
MaryAnn Mish, Chair
Dave Martula
Terri Smith
Allan Zuchowski
Elizabeth Vachula

"350 x 24" Hadley Artist Exhibit
Jane Nevin-Smith
John Romanski
Steve Wilda
Elizabeth Wilda

Founders Day
Gerry Devine

Mt. Holyoke Hikes
Gini Traub, DCR

Calendar and Publications
Marla Miller
Claire Carlson
Mary Thayer
Kathy Tudryn

Souvenirs
Wayne Buckhout, Co-Chair
Sandi Buckhout, Co-Chair
Elaine Tudryn
Joanne Keller
Andrea Goguen
Sarah Wanczyk

Souvenir Store Volunteers
Helen Baj
Joanne Walrath
Martha Boisvert
Marjorie Barstow
Kathy Tudryn
Jane Wagenbach Booth
Brenda Tudryn
Rosalie Weinberg
Carolyn Hayes
Urshula Wood
Pat Osip
Caryn Perley
Cynthia Wade
Bob Page
Gerry Harvey

Fundraising
Joyce West
Dave Moskin
Dave Martula
Mary Thayer
John Vassallo

Website
Rick Thayer
Mary Thayer
Dan Thayer

Design
Paul Benjamin and Marian Chapman, The Benjamin Company

Hopkins Student Council Contact
Katie Brewer

Girl Scout Contact
Kelly Dwight

Hopkins Alumni Association Events
Bernie Wyman
Connie Mieczkowski

Hadley Village Music
Polly Keener

Lecture Series
Hadley Historical Commission:
Marla Miller, Co-Chair
Claire Carlson, Co-Chair
Margaret Miller
Margaret Freeman
Margaret Tudryn
Mitzi Sawada
Tom McGee
Meghan Gelardi Holmes
Brett Johnson
Ginger Goldsbury

First Congregational Church Anniversary Committee
Rev. Sarah Buteux
Lisa West
Shari Parsons
Lauri Osip
Rick Ward

Videographers
Patrick Serio
Walter Mantani
Andrew Morris-Friedman

Amherst Parade Float
Joe Boisvert
Kristen Styspeck
Mary Thayer
Rick Thayer
Gerry Devine
Pete Laurenza
Mark Uchneat

Farmers
Montgomery Rose
North Hadley Sugar Shack
UMass Hadley Farm
Barstow's Longview Farm and Store
Hartsbrook School
Wanczyk Evergreen Nursery
Long Hollow Bison Farm
Hibbard Farm
Mapleline Farm
Astarte Farm
Lakeside U-Pick Strawberries
Great Meadow Fruits
Hartsbrook Farm
Plainville Farm
Twin Oaks Farm
Cook Farm & Flayvors of Cook Farm
The Food Bank Farm

Artists
Neil Broome
Lewis Bryden
Louise Currin
Rick Dec
Rita Edelman
Jacob Elmets
Beth Epstein
Nancy Fernald
Jerry Gabriel
Nadine Gallo
John Gnatek
Patricia Czepiel Hayes
Barbara Johnson
Mare Lyn Judah
Robin Keller
Karen Leveille
Donna McGee
Diane Nevinsmith
Sandra Pipczynski
Kim Rand
Helen Rodak

John Romanski
Rick Thayer
Elizabeth Wilda
Fred Wilda
Steve Wilda
The many participants in the Photo Contest in the Summit House

GARDENERS
Debbie Windoloski
Frank and Joanne Wilda
Irene Bercume
Betsy Alden
Jim and Gerry Harvey
Gene Hoynoski
Rebecca and Mark Uchneat
Sally and Michael Farnham
Jacqui Zuzgo
Mary Thayer
Susan Russell

LECTURERS
Lisa West
Alice Nash
Jim Freeman
Stephen Jendrysik
John Skibiski
Sonia Waskiewicz Chapnick
Stanley Fil
Joseph Pelis
Frank Zalot, Jr.
Stas Radosz
Kevin Sweeney
Rita Reinke
Ed Hood
John Nelson
Bridget Marshall
Brian Ogilvie
Jeffrey Mish

Mary Thayer
Allan Zuchowski
Joseph Zgrodnik
Siobhan Hart
Alice Nash
Bonnie Parsons

TOWN OF HADLEY
Town of Hadley Select Board
Town of Hadley Town Hall staff:
    David Nixon
    Barbara Meehan
    Connie Mieczkowski
    Gail Weiss
    Jessica Spanknebel
    Tim Neyhart
Town of Hadley Highway Dept.
Town of Hadley Police Dept.
Town of Hadley Fire Dept.

PHOTOGRAPHERS
Rick Thayer
Mary Thayer
Dan Thayer
Josh Thayer
Jessica Thayer
Jerry Gabriel
Gerry Delisle
Ray Spezeski
Debbie Windoloski
Jessica Spanknebel
Steve Wilda
Marge Barrett-Mills
MaryAnn Mish
Patsy Lewis
Oscar Edelman
Sandra Pipczynski

OTHER
Janel Beaulieu, TD Banknorth
Janet Selavka

Jennifer Lapis, U.S. Fish & Wildlife
Ted McQueston
Jane Babcock, Goodwin Library
Cathy Zatyrka, Park and Rec.
Young Men's Club
Hadley's American Legion
Hadley Historical Society
The Farm Museum
The Porter-Phelps-Huntington House
Hockanum Villager's Association
Teddy Mieczkowski

AUTHORS
Marla Miller
James Freeman
Eric Freeman
Fred Oakley
Tom Pelissier
Alice Nash
Siobhan Hart
Elizabeth Chilton
Christopher Donta
Edward Hood
Rita Reinke
Douglas Wilson
Martin Antonetti
Bridget Marshall
Brian Ogilvie
Laurel Thatcher Ulrich
Lynne Bassett
Karen Parsons
Gregory Nobels
Stephen Sears
Peter Hardin
Andrea Olmstead
Ethan Carr
Hadley Historical Commission

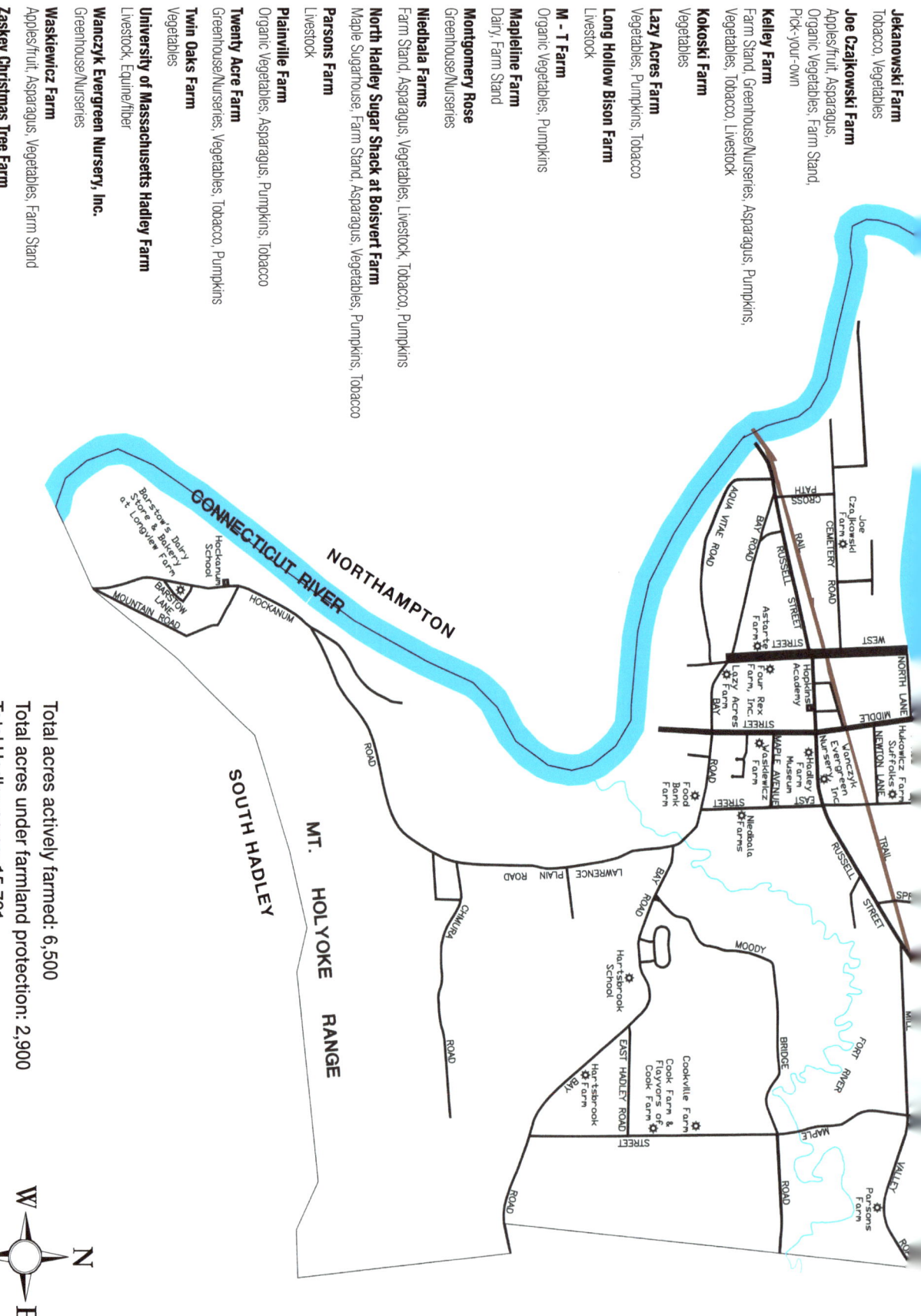

Jekanowski Farm
Tobacco, Vegetables

Joe Czajkowski Farm
Apples/fruit, Asparagus, Organic Vegetables, Farm Stand, Pick-your-own

Kelley Farm
Farm Stand, Greenhouse/Nurseries, Asparagus, Pumpkins, Vegetables, Tobacco, Livestock

Kokoski Farm
Vegetables

Lazy Acres Farm
Vegetables, Pumpkins, Tobacco

Long Hollow Bison Farm
Livestock

M - T Farm
Organic Vegetables, Pumpkins

Mapleline Farm
Dairy, Farm Stand

Montgomery Rose
Greenhouse/Nurseries

Niedbala Farms
Farm Stand, Asparagus, Vegetables, Livestock, Tobacco, Pumpkins

North Hadley Sugar Shack at Boisvert Farm
Maple Sugarhouse, Farm Stand, Asparagus, Vegetables, Pumpkins, Tobacco

Parsons Farm
Livestock

Plainville Farm
Organic Vegetables, Asparagus, Pumpkins, Tobacco

Twenty Acre Farm
Greenhouse/Nurseries, Vegetables, Tobacco, Pumpkins

Twin Oaks Farm
Vegetables

University of Massachusetts Hadley Farm
Livestock, Equine/fiber

Wanczyk Evergreen Nursery, Inc.
Greenhouse/Nurseries

Waskiewicz Farm
Apples/fruit, Asparagus, Vegetables, Farm Stand

Zaskey Christmas Tree Farm
Christmas Trees

Ziomek Farm
Vegetables, Pumpkins, Tobacco

by Randy Izer

Total acres actively farmed: 6,500
Total acres under farmland protection: 2,900
Total Hadley acres: 15,791

Hadley 1659-2009
350 YEARS

AGRICULTURAL MAP 2009

Allard Farm
Dairy

Astarte Farm
Organic Vegetables

Barstow's Dairy Store & Bakery at Longview Farm
Dairy, Farm Stand, Livestock

Brown & Regan LLC
Shade Tobacco

Cook Farm & Flayvors of Cook Farm
Dairy, Farm Stand, Ice Cream

Cookville Farm
Livestock

Devine Farm, Inc.
Dairy, Tobacco, Farm Stand, Greenhouse/Nurseries

Food Bank Farm
Farm Stand, Organic Vegetables, Apples/fruit

Fort River Farm
Livestock

Four Rex Farm, Inc.
Greenhouse/Nurseries, Pumpkins, Vegetables, Farm Stand

Hadley Farm Museum
208 Middle Street

Hadley Garden Center
285 Russell Street, Rt. 9

Hartsbrook Farm
Dairy

Hartsbrook School
Farm Camp

Hibbard Farm
Asparagus, Vegetables

Hukowicz Farm Suffolks
Livestock, Pumpkins

J & J Farms, Waskiewicz Family

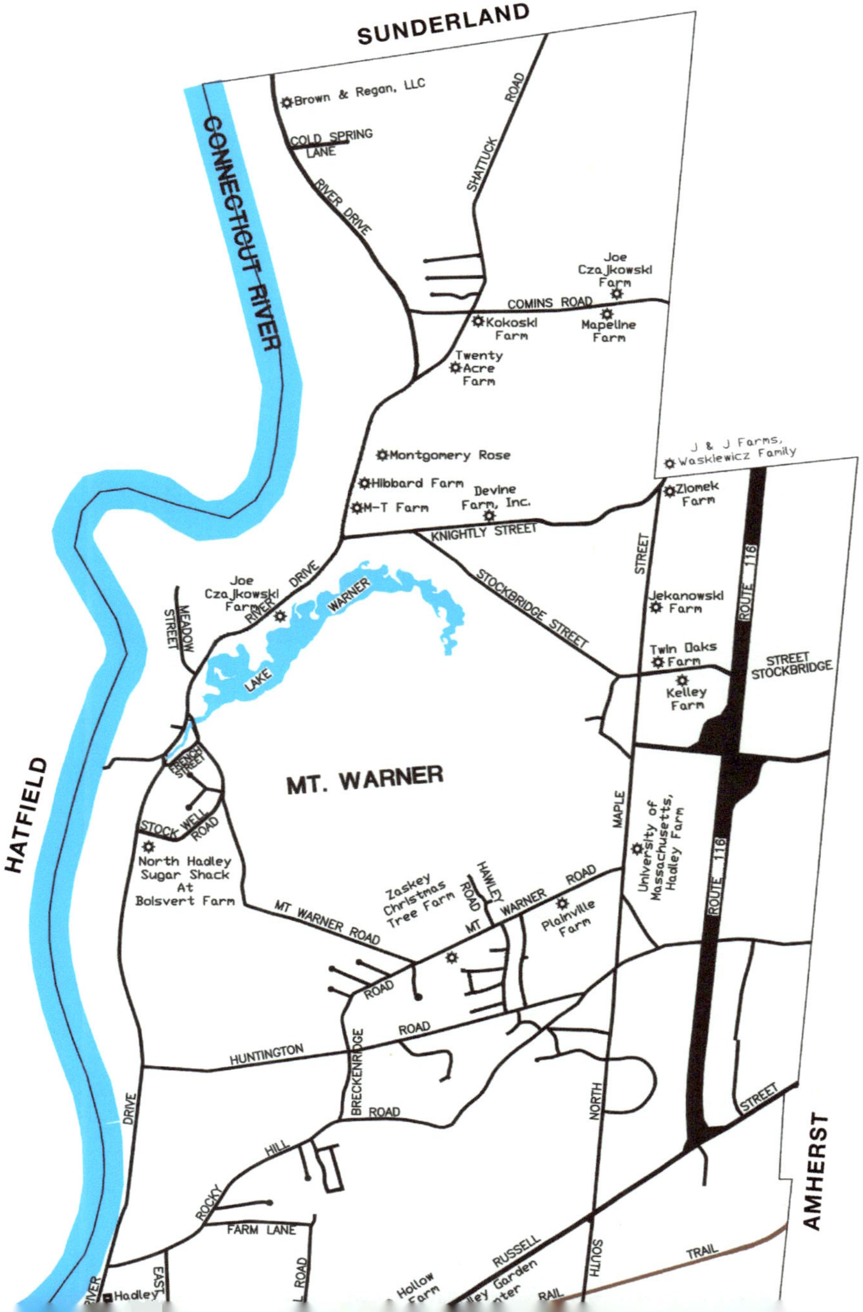

CELEBRATE

Happy 350th Birthday Hadley!

We are celebrating your past and embracing your future.

Our commitment to the community is at the heart of everything we do.
It has been that way since our founding in 1869.

Banking that fits your life perfectly.

bankesb.com | 413.527.4111

Belchertown | Easthampton | Hadley | Northampton
South Hadley | Southampton | Westfield

Member FDIC
Member DIF

You make us feel young!
(We're only 136 years old.)

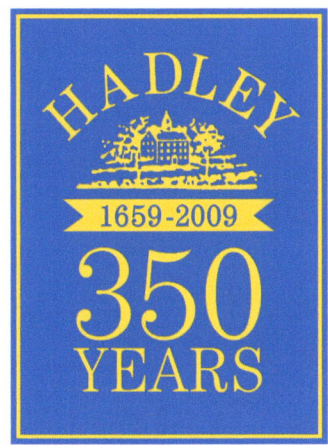

Happy Anniversary Hadley!

Partners in Our Hometown
Florence Savings Bank
Connecting All Offices: 413-586-1300
Route 9 & South Maple Street, Hadley

Member FDIC/Member DIF

florencesavings.com

Happy 350th Anniversary.

We were proud to be a Platinum sponsor and to celebrate the unique heritage that makes Hadley such a special community.

Great relationships start here.

Howard Karger, Photographer: Summit House, Skinner State Park, Hadley
413.538.9500 bankatpeoples.com Member FDIC/Member DIF

Historically great advertising and public relations since 1979

THE BENJAMIN COMPANY

Hadley Crossing
2 Bay Road • Suite 200
Hadley • 413-585-1600

The Cat's Cradle Country Shoppe
Featuring "Olde New England" Country Décor

265 Hadley St {Rte 47}
South Hadley, MA 01075
413-532-4943
Wed~Sat 10-5, Sunday 12~5
{Call for seasonal hours}

Wayne and Sandi Buckhout

"proprietors and gatherers of needful things for the country home"

www.FourSeasonsWine.com

Four Seasons
WINE • LIQUOR • CIGARS

Route 9   **584-8174**

Congratulations Hadley on a great 350th year from

Devine Overhead Doors

Gerry, Denise, Patrick and Kelley Devine

CONGRATULATIONS TO THE TOWN OF HADLEY ON ITS 350TH BIRTHDAY!

Fee-Only Financial Planning

David T. Martula, MBA, MAT, CFP®
277 Bay Road
Hadley, MA 01035
(413) 586-8002
david@martula.com

Congratulations to the Town of Hadley

from Joanne M. Goding,
Hadley resident, Co-owner of Moss Nutrition
& great, great, great, great,
great, great, great, great,
granddaughter of Nathaniel Dickinson —
one of the Original Founders
of the Town of Hadley

Moss Nutrition • 2 Bay Road, Suite 102
Hadley, MA 01035
www.mossnutrition.com

Tools for True Healing™

Distributors of Quality Nutritional Products — exclusively available through healthcare professionals.
Partners in health education for nutrition and lifestyle.
Educational seminars, consultations, and diagnostic expertise.

WORKING TOGETHER
FOR A COMMON GOAL

Investing in a Shared Future.

Making a Difference Together

We're proud to be a part of the Hadley community, especially after an unforgettable 350th Anniversary Celebration!

TD Bank

America's Most Convenient Bank®

1-888-751-9000 | www.tdbank.com

 TD Bank, N.A.

Congratulations

Most Holy Redeemer Catholic Church
120 Russell Street (Rt. 9)
PO Box 375
Hadley, MA 01035
413-584-1326

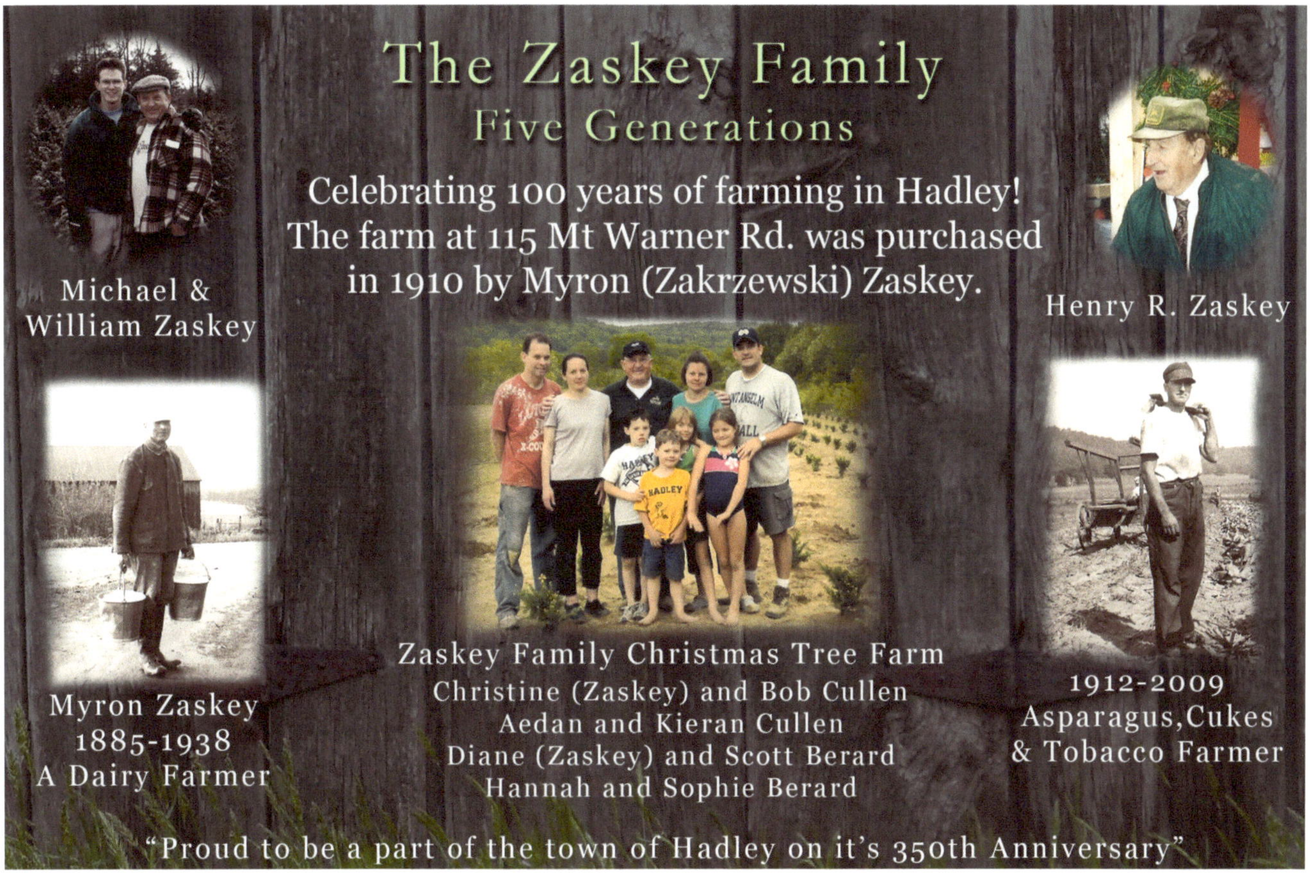

The Zaskey Family
Five Generations

Celebrating 100 years of farming in Hadley! The farm at 115 Mt Warner Rd. was purchased in 1910 by Myron (Zakrzewski) Zaskey.

Michael & William Zaskey

Henry R. Zaskey

Myron Zaskey
1885-1938
A Dairy Farmer

Zaskey Family Christmas Tree Farm
Christine (Zaskey) and Bob Cullen
Aedan and Kieran Cullen
Diane (Zaskey) and Scott Berard
Hannah and Sophie Berard

1912-2009
Asparagus, Cukes & Tobacco Farmer

"Proud to be a part of the town of Hadley on it's 350th Anniversary"

THE MORTGAGE YOU ALWAYS WANTED FOR THE HOME YOU ALWAYS WANTED

NEW No Fee Mortgage PLUS

- $0 APPLICATION FEE
- $0 CLOSING FEES
- + NO PRIVATE MORTGAGE INSURANCE
- + CLOSE-ON-TIME SERVICE GUARANTEE
- + BEST VALUE GUARANTEE

To apply, or to learn more, contact a Bank of America mortgage specialist:

Rochelle Stellato
Mortgage Loan Officer
Phone: 413.787.8682
Fax: 413.787.8023
1 Monarch Place
Springfield, MA 01144

Bank of America
Mortgage

Credit and collateral subject to approval. Only for Bank of America customers. Program, rate, terms and conditions are subject to change without notice. Bank of America, N.A. Equal Housing Lender ©2007 Bank of America Corporation.

ROUTE 9 Diner Restaurant — an American Classic
458-11 Russell Street
Hadley, Ma 01035
Phone: 413.253.0505

Happy Anniversary!

The Dowd Insurance Agencies Congratulate the Town of Hadley on its 350th Anniversary.

THE DOWD AGENCIES
INSURANCE • EMPLOYEE BENEFITS

Holyoke • Amherst • Southampton

800-542-0131 • 413-538-7444

www.dowd.com

THE ALUMNI ASSOCIATION OF HOPKINS ACADEMY

congratulates the Town of Hadley on its 350th Anniversary

Thank you **350th Committee** for all of your hard work!

IT'S BEEN A WONDERFUL CELEBRATION!

Supporting people and their communities

THE BANK OF WESTERN MASSACHUSETTS
salutes

The Town of Hadley on their 350th Anniversary

The Bank of Western Massachusetts

A division of People's United Bank

©2010 People's United Bank Member FDIC

"Happy to Call Hadley My Home!"

Congratulations on 350 Years!

Joyce Fill, REALTOR®
ABR, CRS, GRI, SRES, LMC

Serving Your Real Estate Needs for Nearly 25 Years!

Jones Group REALTORS®
JoyceFill@JonesRealtors.com
www.JoyceFill.com
Cell: 413.531.3675

Happy Birthday Credit Unions!

UMassFive was pleased to honor two major birthdays in 2009. As the Town of Hadley proudly celebrated 350 years, the Credit Union Movement celebrated 100. If it weren't for both Hadley and the Credit Union Movement, UMassFive College Credit Union wouldn't be all that it is today. We have worked to grow our business here and expand the benefits of a not-for-profit financial cooperative to more people throughout our community.

UMassFIVE
COLLEGE
FEDERAL CREDIT UNION

800.852.5886 • umassfive.org

CONGRATULATIONS HADLEY ON YOUR 350TH ANNIVERSARY

John W. Scibak
State Representative

PROUD to be a part of your **LEGACY**.
EXCITED to be a part of your **FUTURE**.

Serving Hadley and the surrounding area for over 50 Years!

Amherst – 549-3700
Belchertown – 323-7295
Northampton – 585-0400

KARL'S EXCAVATING & KARL'S SITE WORK, INC.

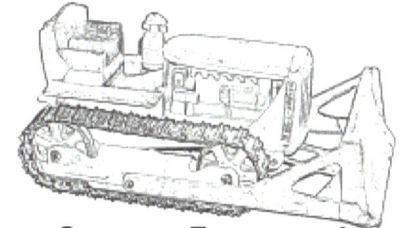

COMPLETE EXCAVATING &
SITE WORK SERVICES
SEWER • WATER • DRAINAGE
SEPTIC SYSTEMS • LOAM • GRAVEL
FILL • TRUCKING • SEWER RODDING
SEPTIC TANK PUMPING
TITLE 5 INSPECTION
COMMERCIAL & RESIDENTIAL

327 RIVER DRIVE
HADLEY, MA 01035
413-549-5396
WWW.KARLSSITEWORK.COM

Kieras Oil, Inc.

SERVING THE HADLEY COMMUNITY FOR THE LAST 60 YEARS WITH:

HEATING OIL, DIESEL FUELS, BOILERS, AIR CONDITIONING, SERVICE & MAINTENANCE

97 RUSSELLVILLE RD. • AMHERST • (413) 549-1144

Fresh, Local and Natural Milk Since 1904

Happy 350th Hadley!

- Family owned and operated
- rBST free
- Our Jersey cows produce a milk that is higher in calcium, protein and milk-fat solids that give it a longer lasting, full flavor taste!

Available in various grocers, food markets and co-ops across the Pioneer Valley and at your door step!

73 Comins Road, Hadley
Home delivery: 413.548.9107
Wholesale or product locations: 413.549.6174

www.maplelinefarm.com

Congratulations, Hadley!

Michael J. Murphy
PARTNER
• 272 Exchange Street • Chicopee, MA 01013 •
413-592-6106

HAPPY BIRTHDAY HADLEY!!!

181 River Drive, Hadley, MA 01035
413-585-8820

www.northhadleysugarshack.com

Congratulations to the people and town of Hadley for 350 years of historic contributions to our American story.

Joan & Ed Smola

We are proud to have established the first dental practice in Hadley over 40 years ago and are grateful to have earned the trust and confidence of our extended family of patients and friends.

My associates and I thank you for the opportunity to serve the dental needs of a new generation of the Hadley community.

Edward H Smola DMD
63 East Street, Hadley
413-584-6557

Congratulations Hadley!

Helen Bemben Szymanowicz 1913-2007
Anne Sarna Kochan 1912-2008
Catherine Drozdal Kusek 1912-2004

Hadley Friends Forever!

Professional Computer Service

valleycomputerworks.com

Rt. 9 Hadley – 587-2666

"Best Computer Service in the Valley since 1999"

Your source for NEWS, ARTS & ENTERTAINMENT

Valley Advocate | Preview Massachusetts
VALLEYADVOCATE.COM

115 Conz Street | P.O. Box 477 | Northampton, MA | 413.529.2840

Wanczyk Nursery

166 Russell Street, Hadley MA, 01035
413.584.3709
customerservice@wanczyknursery.com
www.wanczyknursery.com

We are the growers, come to the source!

COWLS BUILDING SUPPLY

413.549.0001
Fax 413.549.4686
125 Sunderland Rd.
N. Amherst, MA 01059

www.cowls.com

CONNECT
WITH YOUR COMMUNITY

Proudly serving **HADLEY** ...
yesterday, today and tomorrow!

DAILY HAMPSHIRE GAZETTE
GAZETTENET.com

CALL **586-1925** FOR HOME DELIVERY

Internet Strategies Consulting Firm

413.586.1192
Toll Free
866.4.Dot.Inc

Specializing in custom web site
Design - Hosting - Marketing

Web Site Design & Development • Managed Hosting Solutions • Nationwide Internet Access • Computer Systems Consulting & Support • Internet Marketing Initiatives • Online Technology Ventures

www.dotinc.com

esselon cafe
coffee roastery & kitchen

BREAKFAST - BRUNCH - LUNCH - DINNER

ARTISAN COFFEE ROASTER

esselon.com
413.585.1515

99 Russell Street • Hadley, MA 01035

COURTYARD Marriott

423 Russell Street
Hadley
413-256-5454

meetings ~ weddings ~ guestrooms
hampshirehospitality.com

Hadley Garden Center
Everything you need to make your garden grow.
Since 1963

THE HADLEY LIONS CLUB
PROUD SPONSOR OF THE 350ᵀᴴ CELEBRATION
Meeting 1ˢᵀ AND 3ᴿᴰ Thursdays 07:00 PM
HICKORY RIDGE C.C.
WE SERVE OUR COMMUNITY

Clarity of Thought, Warmth of Heart, Strength of Purpose

The Hartsbrook School
| A Waldorf School in the Pioneer Valley

EARLY CHILDHOOD THROUGH HIGH SCHOOL EDUCATION
www.hartsbrook.org 413.584.3198

Kate Carney Iles
Realtor
Accredited Buyers Representative
Senior Real Estate Specialist

delaprealestate.com
kateiles@delaprealestate.com

158 North King Street
Northampton, MA 01060
Office: 413-586-9111 x108
Cell: 413-531-1161

LOCAL NEWS.
LOCAL ADVERTISING.

WE KEEP YOU INFORMED ABOUT WHAT MATTERS MOST.

That's why 77% of adults in Hampden and Hampshire counties rely on The Republican and MassLive.com for local news and information.*

Call 413-788-1100 for home delivery of The Republican

The Republican. |

*Source Scarborough Spring 2008

Happy Birthday, Hadley

Dr. Mark M. Klepacki

190 Russell Street
Hadley, MA 01035

Restorative Dentistry

Telephone: (413) 586-3306   Fax: (413) 586-8847

Thank you for your patronage

Frederick C. Wilda
Helen A. Rodak
P.O Box 427
Hadley, MA 01035
413.586.6691

MINERAL ART SPECIMENS

Nature's Finest Creations

www.naturesfinestcreations.com
E-mail: info@naturesfinestcreations.com

NORM'S AUTO BODY

ESTABLISHED 1964

"IF WE DO IT IT'S DONE RIGHT"
"EXPERT PAINTING AND FENDER WORK"

"Home of the Unbenders"

11 RAILROAD ST
HADLEY, MA 01035
413-586-2824   FAX 584-1264

RS #3443   WWW.NORMSAUTOBODY.COM

FRAME STRAIGHTENING • INSURANCE ESTIMATES

North Star
Self-Directed Learning for Teens

is happy to be a part of
Hadley's educational history!

Learning is natural. School is optional.

www.northstarteens.org   (413) 582-0193

River Drive Auto-Body
81 River Drive
Hadley, Mass. 01035

Complete Auto-Body Service
We Will Work With All Insurance Companies
Satisfaction Guaranteed
413-586-9864

Owner: Steve Szymkowicz   R.S. # 2530

THAYERCARE, INC.
ADULT DAY HEALTH CENTER

Betty Thayer, R.N., Director

49 Middle Street, Hadley, MA 01035
phone: 413-584-0300   fax: 413-584-1684
email: bthayer@thayercare.com

www.ingramcontent.com/pod-product-compliance
Lightning Source LLC
Chambersburg PA
CBHW041122300426
44113CB00002B/34